365 Bible Devotions for Kids

Fun Daily Lessons, Activities, and Simple Scriptures to Grow in Faith

Welcome Aboard, Check Out This Limited-Time Free Bonus!

Ahoy, reader! Welcome to the Ahoy Publications family, and thanks for snagging a copy of this book! Since you've chosen to join us on this journey, we'd like to offer you something special.

Check out the link below for a FREE e-book filled with delightful facts about American History.

But that's not all - you'll also have access to our exclusive email list with even more free e-books and insider knowledge. Well, what are ye waiting for? Click the link below to join and set sail toward exciting adventures in American History.

Access your bonus here

https://ahoypublications.com/

Or, Scan the QR code!

Table of Contents

Introduction

You are about to begin an exciting adventure. This book will be your guide for the next 365 days, helping you discover amazing truths from God's Word, the Bible.

Each day, you will find a new lesson, a simple Bible verse to read, and a fun activity or question. These daily moments will help you learn more about God, understand His great love for you, and grow stronger in your faith.

God wants to talk with you and show you wonderful things. Get ready to open your heart and mind to His wisdom.

Chapter 1: God Made Everything!

"In the beginning God created the heavens and the earth." - Genesis 1:1

Before anything else existed, before the first dawn, before a single grain of sand, God spoke, and everything began. In the verses that follow (Genesis 1 : 2-31), His words shape each new day: light chases away darkness; the wide sky stretches over swirling waters; dry land rises ready for plants to sprout; sun, moon, and stars appear to mark time; birds fill the sky and fish fill the seas; animals roam the land; and, finally, God crafts humans in His own image. Every scene shows that God alone brings order from emptiness and beauty from nothingness. And because the same Creator called *you* into being, your life, like the world around you, has purpose, care, and His constant attention.

Just as Genesis repeats the rhythm "And God saw that it was good," we learn that creation wasn't only powerful, it was *intentional,* friendly, and fit for flourishing. God's delight in His work means He delights in you, too. When He rests on the seventh day (Genesis 2 : 2-3), He sets a pattern for us: pause to enjoy what He has provided, honor His gift of time, and remember that our worth doesn't come from constant activity but from being part of His "very good" creation.

 # ACTIVITY

Go outside or look out a window. Find three things that show God's amazing creativity. Maybe it is the pattern on a leaf, the color of a flower, or a cloud shaped like an animal. Thank God for making these things.

 # PRAYER

Dear God, thank You for creating everything. You are so powerful and wise. Help me to see Your hand in the world around me. Amen.

Chapter 2: Light and Darkness

"God called the light 'day,' and the darkness he called 'night.' And there was evening, and there was morning—the first day." - Genesis 1:5

On the very first day of creation, God looked into a world that was "formless and empty, with darkness over the surface of the deep" (Genesis 1 : 2). Into that pitch-black silence He spoke a single, powerful sentence: "Let there be light." Instantly, brightness burst forth where there had been none.

Next, God separated the light from the darkness. This wasn't just a clever trick; it was God's very first act of *ordering* creation. He named the light "day" and the darkness "night," giving them each a purpose and a boundary. From that moment on, time itself began ticking, evening and morning, the first day (Genesis 1 : 5). Every sunrise you watch and every bedtime you count on still follow the schedule God set up here.

Notice, too, that God didn't eliminate darkness; He *ruled over* it by keeping it within limits. When life feels confusing or scary, this creation story reminds us that God can organize our "dark" places just as easily as He organized the universe. Because He is a God of order and beauty, we can trust Him to bring light, structure, and purpose to every part of our lives.

 **ACTIVITY**

Think about your favorite time of day. Is it a bright morning or a quiet night?

Draw a picture of something you enjoy doing during that time. Remember that God made both day and night for us.

PRAYER

Heavenly Father, thank You for giving us day and night. Thank You for light that helps us see and for rest that comes with darkness. Amen.

Chapter 3: Sky and Water

"And God said, 'Let there be a vault between the waters to separate water from water.' So God made the vault and separated the water under the vault from the water above it. And it was so. God called the vault 'sky.' And there was evening, and there was morning— the second day." - Genesis 1:6-8

On the second day of creation, God spoke again, saying, "Let there be a vault between the waters to separate water from water" (Genesis 1 : 6). At His command, an invisible ceiling, what the Bible calls the "expanse", formed. This vast space we call the sky divided the waters below (the oceans, rivers, and lakes) from the waters above (the moisture that gathers into clouds). From that moment on, the atmosphere became earth's protective blanket: it carries oxygen for every breath you take, filters the sun's fierce rays, and holds the rain that waters crops and fills streams. When you look up and see birds gliding or clouds drifting like giant ships, remember that each layer of sky is part of God's careful blueprint.

God's separation of the waters also set the stage for the water cycle that still sustains life today. Evaporation lifts water into the air, condensation forms clouds, and precipitation returns it to the ground. Scientists spend entire careers studying this elegant system, yet Genesis shows us that its designer completed it with a single word. That means the One who orders wind patterns and rainfall can certainly bring order to our lives as well. When things feel scattered or uncertain, we can trust the God who planned every cloud and current to guide us with the same wisdom and precision.

 **ACTIVITY**

Look at the sky today. Are there clouds? Is it blue? Imagine how big God is to create such a huge sky. Now, draw the sky that you see.

PRAYER

God, You made the amazing sky. Thank You for its beauty and for the clouds that bring rain to the earth. Amen.

Chapter 4: Land, Seas, and Plants

"Then God said, 'Let the land produce vegetation: seed-bearing plants and trees on the land that bear fruit with seed in it, according to their various kinds.' And it was so." - Genesis 1:11

God spoke again: "Let the land produce vegetation" (Genesis 1 : 11). All at once the barren ground burst with life. Soft grasses spread like green carpets, tiny seeds cracked open into colorful wildflowers, and sturdy trees shot skyward already loaded with fruit. Each plant came "according to its kind," so apple seeds would always grow more apple trees and wheat kernels would always grow new wheat. In a single command God wrote the recipe for every harvest in history, designing a self-replenishing pantry for people and animals long before either existed.

Think about that the next time you crunch a carrot or kick a soccer ball across fresh grass: every shade of green, every bite of fruit, every seed tucked inside a strawberry traces back to God's Day-Three creativity. He turns emptiness into abundance and chaos into order, proving His wisdom and power in every sprout and every forest on earth.

 # ACTIVITY

Find a plant outside or in your home. Look closely at its leaves stem, and any flowers or fruit. How is it different from other plants you know? Notice the details God put into each one.

 # PRAYER

Creator God, thank You for the land, the seas, and all the plants. Thank You for providing food and beauty through Your creation. Amen.

Chapter 5: Sun, Moon, and Stars

"And God said, 'Let there be lights in the vault of the sky to separate the day from the night, and let them serve as signs to mark sacred times, and days and years, and let them be lights in the vault of the sky to give light on the earth.' And it was so." - Genesis 1:14-15

On the fourth day of creation, God filled the vault of the sky with three kinds of "lights." First He set the sun to blaze during the hours of daylight, bathing the earth in warmth and energy that keeps plants growing and hearts beating. Then He arranged the moon to glow by reflected light, ruling the night and tugging gently on the seas to guide the tides. Finally, He scattered uncountable stars across the black canvas of space: great burning spheres so distant they appear as pinpricks, yet together they form constellations that have helped people navigate and wonder at God's greatness for thousands of years.

These lights do more than brighten the sky. God assigned them to "mark sacred times, and days and years." When the sun reaches its highest point, we call it noon; when the moon completes its phases, a month has passed; when the earth finishes its lap around the sun, a year is complete. Even the changing constellations signal new seasons for planting and harvest. By anchoring time itself to the dependable rhythm of heavenly bodies, God showed that He rules over calendars and clocks just as surely as He rules over oceans and mountains. Every sunrise is a reminder that His mercies are new each morning, and every star-studded night whispers that His promises endure as long as the lights in the heavens remain.

Because the Creator has woven such order into the cosmos, we can trust Him to bring order to our own schedules and seasons of life. Whether you are rushing through a busy day or lying awake beneath a quiet sky, remember that the same God who numbered the stars is guiding the minutes and years of your story with purpose and care.

 ACTIVITY

Look at the sky tonight. Can you see the moon or any stars? If it's daytime, imagine the sun shining brightly. Draw your favorite celestial body (sun, moon, or stars).

PRAYER

Dear God, thank You for the sun, moon, and stars. They show Your greatness and light up our world. Amen.

Chapter 6: Fish and Birds

"And God said, 'Let the water teem with living creatures, and let birds fly above the earth across the vault of the sky.' So God created the great creatures of the sea and every living thing with which the water teems and that moves about in it, according to their kinds, and every winged bird according to its kind. And God saw that it was good." - Genesis 1:20-21

On the fifth day of creation, God turned silent seas and empty skies into vibrant habitats bursting with movement. At His word, the oceans swarmed with every kind of swimmer, from microscopic plankton to graceful dolphins and giants like blue whales. Overhead, the first wingbeats sliced through the air as hummingbirds hovered, gulls swooped, and eagles soared on rising currents. Each creature appeared "according to its kind," meaning God built in the ability for fish to lay more fish eggs and birds to hatch more birds, ensuring that life on Earth would keep flourishing without running out.

This is also the first time Genesis records God blessing living beings: He told them to multiply and fill their realms. That blessing reveals His delight in a world brimming with life and sound: splashing fins, chorusing seabirds, rippling schools that paint silver patterns beneath the waves. Every fin, feather, and tide testifies that the Creator loves abundance and designs with purpose, inviting us to marvel at His artistry and care for the living world He entrusted to us.

 # ACTIVITY

Think about your favorite fish or bird. What makes it special? Maybe it's a colorful fish or a bird that sings a beautiful song. Try to make the sound of your favorite bird.

 # PRAYER

God, thank You for all the fish in the sea and all the birds in the sky. Your creation is amazing! Amen.

Chapter 7: Animals and People

"Then God said, 'Let us make mankind in our image, in our likeness, so that they may rule over the fish in the sea and the birds in the sky, over the livestock and all the wild animals, and over all the creatures that move along the ground.' So God created mankind in his own image, in the image of God he created them; male and female he created them." - Genesis 1:26-27

On the sixth day, the land suddenly came alive. At God's command, herds thundered across plains, curious meerkats popped out of burrows, and lumbering elephants shook the ground with each step. Every creature instantly knew how to eat, run, play, and raise young, evidence of a Designer who programs instincts as easily as we snap puzzle pieces together.

God saved His most personal work for last. He fashioned human beings in his own image. After giving people life, God handed them a job description: *care for* (not crush) the fish, birds, livestock, and earth itself. Being "in His image" means acting as caretakers the way a gardener tends a beautiful park that doesn't belong to him. When we recycle, protect habitats, treat pets kindly, or invent tools that help others thrive, we echo that original assignment.

Most amazing of all, the God who spins galaxies also desires a relationship with us. The same voice that called mammals into being is the voice that invites you to talk with Him, learn from Him, and share His love with the world He entrusted to your care.

 **ACTIVITY**

Look in a mirror. Remember that you are made in God's image. What is one way you can show kindness to an animal or care for a plant today?

PRAYER

Loving God, thank You for making me and all the animals. Thank You for making me special, in Your image. Help me to care for Your world. Amen.

Chapter 8: God Rested

"By the seventh day God had finished the work he had been doing; so on the seventh day he rested from all his work. Then God blessed the seventh day and made it holy, because on it he rested from all the work of creating that he had done." - Genesis 2:2-3

After six exciting days of shaping oceans, lighting stars, and breathing life into every corner of the earth, God paused. His "rest" wasn't because He was tired (God never runs out of energy) but to celebrate the goodness of all He had made and to set apart a special rhythm for His creation. By blessing the seventh day and calling it holy, He wrapped it like a present and handed it to people as a reward for a week well spent: six days of meaningful work followed by a day of joyful rest.

That Sabbath rest is not permission to be lazy; it is an invitation to stop chasing and start praising. When we set aside ordinary chores and schoolwork for one day, we're saying, "God, I trust You to keep the world spinning while I slow down." It's a day to breathe, enjoy family, worship together, walk in His creation, and let our hearts refill so we can serve Him with fresh strength in the week ahead. In God's perfect design, hard work and true rest go hand in hand: six days sowing and building, one day savoring and blessing the One who makes it all possible.

 **ACTIVITY**

What is your favorite way to rest? Maybe it is reading a book, playing a quiet game, or taking a nap. Always remember, the sabbath itself is the day of rest and is a reward and gift for working the rest of the time.

 **PRAYER**

Gracious God, thank You for the gift of rest. Help me to remember to take time to rest and to spend time with You. Amen.

Chapter 9: God's Good Creation

"God saw all that he had made, and it was very good." - Genesis 1:31

When God stepped back to survey the universe He had shaped, glittering galaxies, swirling seas, every plant, animal, and person, He didn't just call it "good" as He had six times before. He declared it "very good", a Hebrew phrase that means completely satisfying, exactly right, and overflowing with joyful potential.

Nothing was out of place: lions prowled without harming lambs, flowers bloomed without wilting, people walked with God without fear or shame. The earth pulsed with perfect harmony, a masterpiece that reflected its Maker's flawless character.

This verdict also reveals how God values His creation, including you. When He calls something "very good," He is pronouncing delight, purpose, and worth over it. Your life is not an accident or an afterthought; it fits inside God's larger story of goodness.

Because the Creator still loves what He has made, we are invited to protect His world, celebrate its beauty, and trust that, even when brokenness later enters the scene, God's ultimate plan is to restore everything to that original "very good" peace.

 **ACTIVITY**

Think about something you made or built that you are proud of. How did it feel when you finished it and saw it was good? God felt that way about His whole creation. Draw a picture of your favorite part of God's "very good" creation.

PRAYER

Almighty God, thank You for making such a good and perfect world. Help me to appreciate all the good things You have given us. Amen.

Chapter 10: Adam and Eve

"Then the Lord God made a woman from the rib he had taken out of the man, and he brought her to the man." - Genesis 2:22

God created the first man, Adam, from the dust of the ground and breathed life into him. God caused Adam to fall into a deep sleep, took one of his ribs, and made the first woman, Eve.

Crafting her from Adam's rib (literally "side" in Hebrew) speaks volumes: she was not made from his head to rule over him, nor from his feet to be trampled, but from his side, close to his heart, to stand with him in equal worth and mutual support.

Adam and Eve lived in a perfect garden, and they walked and talked with God. They were the first humans, and God loved them very much.

 ## ACTIVITY

God created Adam and Eve to be companions. Think about a good friend or family member. What is one thing you appreciate about them? Write it down or tell them.

 ## PRAYER

Dear God, thank You for creating Adam and Eve, and for making us able to have relationships with others. Help me to be a good friend and to love my family. Amen.

Chapter 11: The Garden of Eden

"The Lord God made all kinds of trees grow out of the ground—trees that were pleasing to the eye and good for food. In the middle of the garden were the tree of life and the tree of the knowledge of good and evil." - Genesis 2:9

Before shaping the first human, God had already planted a magnificent garden. Every tree there was both beautiful to look at and delicious to eat, shading winding paths of soft grass. A single river rose in Eden and then split into four mighty streams, Pishon, Gihon, Tigris, and Euphrates, so the garden was constantly watered and overflowing with life.

Only after forming Adam from the dust did God take him **into** this paradise and entrust him with a job: *"to work it and take care of it."* In other words, Eden was never meant to be a lounge for laziness; it was a place where meaningful labor and perfect rest lived side by side. Surrounded by abundance, Adam could harvest fruit without fear of scarcity, study creation without thorns or weeds, and walk in unbroken fellowship with his Creator. Eden's order shows God's thoughtful provision, and Adam's assignment reminds us that real joy comes from partnering with God: cultivating His gifts, protecting His world, and enjoying His presence all at once.

 **ACTIVITY**

Imagine your perfect garden. What kind of trees, flowers, or animals would be there? Draw a picture of your ideal garden, thinking about how wonderful Eden must have been.

PRAYER

Dear God, thank You for the beautiful world You created, like the Garden of Eden. Help me to appreciate and care for the nature around me. Amen.

Chapter 12: God's Command

"And the Lord God commanded the man, 'You are free to eat from any tree in the garden; but you must not eat from the tree of the knowledge of good and evil, for when you eat from it you will certainly die.'" - Genesis 2:16-17

God gave Adam a very important instruction in the Garden of Eden. He told Adam he was free to eat from any tree in the garden, except for one: the tree of the knowledge of good and evil. God warned Adam that if he ate from that tree, he would surely die. This command was a test of Adam's obedience and trust in God. God gave this rule for Adam's good, to protect him and keep him in a perfect relationship with Him.

 **ACTIVITY**

Think about a rule your parents or teachers have given you that helps keep you safe or helps things run smoothly. How does following that rule show you trust them? Discuss it with a family member.

 **PRAYER**

Heavenly Father, thank You for giving us rules that help us. Please help me to obey Your commands and trust that Your ways are always best. Amen.

Chapter 13: Choosing Our Own Way

"When the woman saw that the fruit of the tree was good for food and pleasing to the eye, and also desirable for gaining wisdom, she took some and ate it. She also gave some to her husband, who was with her, and he ate it." - Genesis 3:6

Life in Eden was full and free. Every tree except one stood open for Adam and Eve to enjoy, because God had already warned, "You must not eat from the tree of the knowledge of good and evil" (Genesis 2:17).

When the serpent entered the scene he used a crafty question to sow doubt. The creature's words opposed God's. He promised Eve she would not die and that eating the fruit would make her "like God, knowing good and evil" (Genesis 3:4–5).

Eve weighed what she saw: the fruit looked good for food, pleasing to the eye, and desirable for gaining wisdom. She chose the serpent's half-truth over God's clear command. She ate and handed some to Adam, who was with her and also ate. In that moment, both of them traded trusting obedience for self-rule.

Their act was not a slip of hunger but a deliberate decision to define right and wrong on their own terms. Genesis records the tragic first step that introduced shame, fear, and brokenness into a once-perfect world, reminding every reader that true freedom is found not in grasping more, but in resting inside the boundaries God sets for our good.

 **ACTIVITY**

Think of a time when it was hard to obey a rule. What happened? How did you feel? Talk about why it is important to choose to obey, even when it is difficult.

 **PRAYER**

Dear God, sometimes it is hard to obey. Please help me to listen to Your voice and choose Your way, even when I am tempted to do something else. Amen.

Chapter 14: Sin Enters the World

"So the Lord God banished him from the Garden of Eden to work the ground from which he had been taken." - Genesis 3:23

When Adam and Eve disobeyed God, something very sad happened. Their perfect relationship with God was broken. This act of disobedience is called sin. Sin separated them from God and brought consequences into the world, like pain, hard work, and eventually death. Because Adam and Eve were the first humans, sin entered the world through them, and it has affected everyone since. This is why we sometimes make wrong choices.

 # ACTIVITY

Think about a time you made a mistake or did something wrong. How did it feel? What did you learn from it? Write down one way you can try to make a better choice next time.

PRAYER

Forgiving God, I am sorry for the times I make wrong choices. Thank You for loving me even when I sin. Help me to choose what is right. Amen.

Chapter 15: God's Sadness

"The Lord God made garments of skin for Adam and his wife and clothed them." - Genesis 3:21

God is perfect and holy. He loves His creation, and He loves people. When Adam and Eve sinned, it made God sad. He did not want them to be separated from Him. God still loved them, even though they had disobeyed. He showed His care by making clothes for them when they realized they were naked. God's sadness over sin shows how much He desires for us to live in close relationship with Him, free from anything that hurts us or Him.

 **ACTIVITY**

Think about a time someone you love was sad because of something you did. How did you try to make it right? God still loved Adam and Eve, even when they made Him sad. Draw a picture of a sad face and then a happy face, thinking about how God wants us to be close to Him.

PRAYER

Loving God, I know my choices can sometimes make you sad. Thank You for Your great love and for always wanting me to be close to You. Help me to bring You joy. Amen.

Chapter 16: A Promise of Hope

"And I will put enmity between you and the woman, and between your offspring and hers; he will crush your head, and you will strike his heel." - Genesis 3:15

Even though Adam and Eve had sinned and were leaving the perfect garden, God did not leave them without hope. He made a promise right away: one day a descendant from the woman's family would crush the serpent's head.

In that single statement God declared that evil would not have the last word. His plan to restore what had been broken was already in motion, reminding us that God always provides a path forward, even when everything feels lost.

 **ACTIVITY**

Imagine you are waiting for a special gift. How does the promise of that gift make you feel? Think about how God's promise of a Savior brought hope to Adam and Eve. Draw a picture of a gift.

PRAYER

Thank You, God, for always giving us hope. Thank You for Your promise of a Savior, Jesus, who defeats evil. Amen.

Chapter 17: God's Love Never Changes

"The Lord God made garments of skin for Adam and his wife and clothed them." — Genesis 3:21

Even after Adam and Eve disobeyed, God's love showed up in a tangible way: He personally fashioned durable clothes to cover their shame and protect them outside the garden. This simple act reminds us that God's care does not end when we fail.

His compassion reaches into our broken moments, meeting real needs while pointing to His desire to restore and walk with us. Whenever we stumble, we can remember the first garments, evidence that God's steady love remains constant, providing help and hope even after our biggest mistakes.

 # ACTIVITY

Think about someone who loves you very much, no matter what. How does their love make you feel safe and happy? Write down three words that describe God's love.

PRAYER

Loving God, thank You that Your love never changes. Thank You for always loving me. Help me to remember Your great love for me today. Amen.

Chapter 18: Caring for Creation

"The Lord God took the man and put him in the Garden of Eden to work it and take care of it." - Genesis 2:15

When God created the world, He gave Adam and Eve a special job: to take care of the Garden of Eden. This means we also have a responsibility to care for the world God made. We can show our love for God by taking good care of the animals, plants, and natural places around us. Picking up litter, saving water, or being kind to animals are ways we can be good stewards of God's creation.

 ACTIVITY

Look around your home or neighborhood. What is one small thing you can do today to care for God's creation? Maybe it is watering a plant, recycling something, or making sure a pet has fresh water. Do that one thing!

 PRAYER

Creator God, thank You for trusting me to care for Your world. Help me to be a good helper and to protect the amazing things You have made. Amen.

Chapter 19: God Sees Everything

"But the Lord God called to the man, 'Where are you?'" — Genesis 3:9

After Adam and Eve ate the forbidden fruit, guilt rushed in and they dove behind the garden's trees, hoping their Creator wouldn't notice. The sound of God walking in the cool of the day told them what is still true for us: God always knows where we are, geographically and spiritually. His question, "Where are you?", wasn't to gather information; it was an invitation to step back into an honest relationship.

That same gentle pursuit continues today. God sees our highs and lows, our courage and our stumbles, and He still calls, "Where are you?" Not to condemn, but to draw us out of hiding and cover us with grace. We can bring Him our fears, failures, and joys, confident that nothing is hidden from His loving eyes and nothing can push Him away from those He created and cherishes.

 # ACTIVITY

Play a quick game of "hide and seek" with a family member. Think about how hard it is to hide from someone who is really good at finding you. Remember that God always sees you, and He is always there.

PRAYER

All-knowing God, thank You that You see me always. Thank You for watching over me and caring for me. Help me to remember You are always near. Amen.

Chapter 20: God Knows Our Names

"Before I formed you in the womb I knew you, before you were born I set you apart." - Jeremiah 1:5

God knows every single person He has created. He knows your name, how many hairs are on your head, and every thought you have. He does not just know about you; He knows *you*. This means you are not just one person in a big world. You are a special individual known and loved by God. This personal knowledge shows how deeply God cares for each of us.

You are a one-of-a-kind masterpiece, carefully designed and deeply cherished by the Creator who understands you better than anyone else ever could.

ACTIVITY

Write your full name on a piece of paper. Think about how special your name is to you and your family. Remember that God knows your name and knows everything about you. Draw a picture of yourself.

PRAYER

Dear God, thank You for knowing me so well. Thank You for knowing my name and for caring about every part of me. Help me to know You more each day. Amen.

Chapter 21: God's Plan for Us

"For I know the plans I have for you,' declares the Lord, 'plans to prosper you and not to harm you, plans to give you hope and a future.'" - Jeremiah 29:11

Jeremiah's promise was first delivered to a very specific audience: Jewish exiles living in Babylon who wondered whether God had abandoned them. Through the prophet, God assured them He still held their future: after seventy years He would bring them home and restore their nation's life and worship. The verse is not a blank check for instant success but a reminder of God's covenant faithfulness even when circumstances look bleak.

That historical setting matters, yet the heart behind the words remains true for all who belong to God. He never designs plans that are ultimately harmful for His people; instead, His larger story always bends toward hope, renewal, and flourishing. We may not see every detail now, but like the exiles we can trust that our present chapter fits into a wider narrative He is writing for the good of those who love Him.

 # ACTIVITY

Think about something you dream of doing or becoming when you grow up. God has a plan for you that is even better! Write down one thing you are excited about for your future.

_____

_____

_____

_____

_____

_____

_____

_____

_____

_____

PRAYER

Loving God, thank You for having a good plan for my life. Help me to trust You and follow Your lead each day. Amen.

Chapter 22: We Are Made in God's Image

"So God created mankind in his own image, in the image of God he created them; male and female he created them." - Genesis 1:27

Being made "in God's image" means every human life, male and female alike, echoes something of the Creator Himself. We are gifted with a moral compass to discern right from wrong, imagination to design and build, emotions to love deeply, and a spirit capable of knowing and worshiping God.

Reflecting His likeness also entrusts us with a royal task: to represent His character on earth by caring for people, animals, and the planet just as He would. Because this divine imprint rests on each person from the moment of life, our worth is not measured by talent, age, or success; it is anchored in God's decision to fashion us after His own heart.

 **ACTIVITY**

Think about a quality you like about yourself, like being kind, creative, or a good listener. How might that quality reflect a little bit of God's character? Draw a picture of yourself doing something you enjoy that uses one of your special qualities.

PRAYER

Wonderful God, thank You for making me in Your image. Help me to use the qualities You have given me to show Your love to others. Amen.

Chapter 23: Our Unique Gifts

"Every good and perfect gift is from above, coming down from the Father of the heavenly lights, who does not change like shifting shadows." - James 1:17

Just as God made each star different and each flower unique, He made each person with special gifts and talents. Some people are good at art, others at sports, some at helping, or at solving problems. These gifts are from God, and He wants us to use them for good. When we use our gifts, we can help others and bring glory to God. Your unique gifts make you special.

 **ACTIVITY**

What is one thing you are good at? It could be anything! Think about how you can use that gift to help someone else or make someone smile today.

 **PRAYER**

God, thank You for giving me unique gifts and talents. Help me to use them to serve You and to bless the people around me. Amen.

Chapter 24: Thanking God for Creation

"The heavens declare the glory of God; the skies proclaim the work of his hands." - Psalm 19:1

We have spent many days thinking about all the wonderful things God created: light, sky, land, plants, sun, moon, stars, fish, birds, animals, and people. All of it is good, and it shows God's power, wisdom, and love. Taking time to thank God for His creation is important. When we appreciate the world around us, we remember how great our God is.

 ## ACTIVITY

Go on a "thankfulness walk" around your house or outside. For every five steps you take, name one thing you see that God created and say "Thank You, God!"

 ## PRAYER

Gracious God, thank You for the beauty of Your creation. Thank You for making a world full of amazing things for us to enjoy. We praise You for Your greatness. Amen.

Chapter 25: God's Power

"For with God nothing will be impossible." - Luke 1:37

When God created the entire universe simply by speaking, it shows His incredible power. He did not need tools or help. He just spoke, and it happened. There is nothing too difficult for God. His power means He can do anything He chooses, and He is strong enough to handle any problem or challenge we face. We can trust in His mighty power.

 **ACTIVITY**

Think about something that seems impossible to you right now. It could be a big challenge at school or a difficult task. Write it down. Remember that God's power is limitless.

_____

_____

_____

_____

_____

_____

_____

_____

_____

_____

_____

_____

PRAYER

Almighty God, thank You for Your amazing power. Help me to remember that nothing is impossible for You. Amen.

Chapter 26: God's Wisdom

"The Lord by wisdom founded the earth; by understanding he established the heavens." - Proverbs 3:19

God did not just create everything; He created it with perfect wisdom. The way the seasons change, how plants grow, or how our bodies work all show God's incredible intelligence. He designed every detail perfectly. God's wisdom means He always knows the best way to do things and the best path for us to take. We can ask Him for wisdom when we need to make choices.

 **ACTIVITY**

Think about something complex that works perfectly, like a clock or a tree growing from a tiny seed. How does that show wisdom? Draw a simple maze and think about how God's wisdom helps us find the right path in life.

PRAYER

Wise God, thank You for Your perfect wisdom in creating the world. Please give me wisdom to make good choices and to understand Your ways. Amen.

Chapter 27: God's Goodness

"The Lord is good to all; he has compassion on all he has made." - Psalm 145:9

Every element of creation emerged flawless, because it came from a flawless Creator. God's character overflows with kindness, generosity, and unerring justice, so His intentions for the world, and for us, always aim toward flourishing.

Hard seasons can blur that truth, but they never alter it. Keeping sight of His unwavering goodness steadies our hearts and grounds our hope.

 **ACTIVITY**

Think about something good that happened to you today or this week. How did it make you feel? Write down one way you can show goodness to someone else today.

_____

_____

_____

_____

_____

_____

_____

_____

_____

_____

PRAYER

Good God, thank You for Your goodness that fills the earth. Help me to see Your goodness in my life and to share Your goodness with others. Amen.

Chapter 28: God's Holiness

And the four living creatures, each by itself severally, had six wings, around and within [are] full of eyes, and rest they have not day and night, saying, `Holy, holy, holy, Lord God Almighty, who was, and who is, and who is coming;'" - Revelation 4:8

God is holy, which means He is completely pure, perfect, and set apart from everything else. There is no sin or evil in Him. His holiness means He is worthy of all our praise and respect. Because God is holy, He cannot be around sin. This is why sin separated us from Him. But God, in His love, made a way for us to be close to Him again.

 # ACTIVITY

Think about something that is very clean and pure, like fresh, clear water. How does that remind you of God's holiness? Draw a crown, thinking about how God is a holy King.

PRAYER

Holy God, You are perfect and pure. Thank You for making a way for me to be close to You. Help me to honor Your holiness in my life. Amen.

Chapter 29: God Is Everywhere

"Where can I go from your Spirit? Where can I flee from your presence?" - Psalm 139:7

God's presence isn't confined to a building or a single spot on the map. Whether you're scaling a mountain, sitting in a crowded classroom, or lying awake in the dark, His Spirit is already there, closer than your next breath.

You could board the fastest rocket, dive to the ocean floor, or hide behind your biggest mistake, and you still wouldn't slip off His radar. That's not meant to make us nervous; it's meant to steady us.

The One who sees every sunrise and midnight also sees you, accompanies you, and whispers guidance when you feel lost. Because His nearness never flickers, you can pray, rejoice, or reach for help at any moment, knowing you're wrapped in a presence that will never let you go.

 **ACTIVITY**

Close your eyes and imagine God's presence all around you, like the air you breathe. Think about how comforting it is that He is always near. Write down three places you have been today, and remember God was there with you in each place.

PRAYER

God, thank You that You are everywhere. Thank You for always being with me and never leaving me alone. Amen.

Chapter 30: God Is Always with Us

"Have I not commanded you? Be strong and courageous. Do not be afraid; do not be discouraged, for the Lord your God will be with you wherever you go." - Joshua 1:9

Because God is everywhere, He is always with us. He walks with us through our day, whether we are playing, learning, or even sleeping. When we feel happy, He is there. When we feel sad or scared, He is there too. We can talk to Him anytime, anywhere, knowing He is listening. This truth gives us courage and peace.

 **ACTIVITY**

Think about a time you felt alone. How would it have felt to know God was right there with you? Draw a picture of yourself doing something, and add a small, simple heart next to it to represent God's presence.

PRAYER

Dear God, thank You for always being with me. Help me to feel Your presence and to remember You are always by my side. Amen.

Chapter 31: God Hears Our Prayers

"This is the confidence we have in approaching God: that if we ask anything according to his will, he hears us." - 1 John 5:14

God is so big and powerful, yet He cares about each of us so much that He listens when we talk to Him. Prayer is simply talking to God. We can tell Him our joys, our worries, our thanks, and our needs. God hears every single prayer, no matter how big or small. He loves to hear from His children.

 ACTIVITY

Find a quiet spot. Close your eyes and tell God something you are thankful for today. Then, tell Him one thing you need help with. Remember, He is listening.

 **PRAYER**

Listening God, thank You for hearing my prayers. Thank You for caring about what I say. Help me to talk with You often. Amen.

Chapter 32: God Answers Our Prayers

"This is the confidence we have in approaching God: that if we ask anything according to His will, He hears us. And if we know that He hears us—whatever we ask—we know that we have what we asked of Him." — 1 John 5 : 14-15

God hears our prayers, and He also answers them. Sometimes He answers with a "yes," and we get exactly what we asked for. Sometimes He answers with a "no," because He knows something better for us, or it is not the right time. Sometimes He answers with "wait," teaching us patience. God's answers are always perfect, because He is wise and good. We can trust His answers, even when they are not what we expected.

 **ACTIVITY**

Think about a time God answered a prayer for you. How did it make you feel? Write down one thing you are praying for right now. Trust God to answer in His perfect way.

PRAYER

God, thank You for answering my prayers. Help me to trust Your wisdom and timing, even when Your answer is different from what I hoped for. Amen.

Chapter 33: Trusting God's Plan

"Trust in the Lord with all your heart and lean not on your own understanding; in all your ways submit to him, and he will make your paths straight." - Proverbs 3:5-6

We learned that God has a plan for us. Sometimes, His plan might seem confusing or difficult. We might not understand why certain things happen. Trusting God's plan means believing that He knows what is best, even when we do not. It means holding onto His goodness and wisdom, knowing He is working everything out for our good and His glory.

 ACTIVITY

Draw a winding path on a piece of paper. Imagine you are walking on it, and you cannot see around the next bend. How does it feel to trust that someone good is leading you? Talk about a time you had to trust someone even when you did not understand.

 PRAYER

Faithful God, it is hard to trust what I cannot see. Help me to trust Your plan for my life, knowing You are always leading me in the best way. Amen.

Chapter 34: God's Patience

"The Lord is compassionate and gracious, slow to anger, abounding in love." - Psalm 103:8

God is very patient with us. He gives us many chances to learn and grow. When Adam and Eve sinned, God did not immediately destroy them. He showed patience. When we make mistakes or struggle to understand something, God does not give up on us. He waits for us, teaches us, and helps us. His patience is a wonderful part of His character.

 **ACTIVITY**

Think about a time you had to be patient with someone or something. How did it feel? What did you learn? Write down one way you can try to be more patient today.

PRAYER

Patient God, thank You for being so patient with me. Help me to learn from my mistakes and to grow closer to You each day. Amen.

Chapter 35: God's Forgiveness

"If we confess our sins, he is faithful and just and will forgive us our sins and purify us from all unrighteousness." - 1 John 1:9

Because God is holy, sin separates us from Him. However, God, in His great love, offers us forgiveness. Forgiveness means God chooses not to hold our sins against us when we are truly sorry and turn to Him. He sent Jesus to make this forgiveness possible. When we ask for forgiveness, God washes away our sin and brings us back into a right relationship with Him. This is an amazing gift.

 # ACTIVITY

Draw a picture of a messy slate or whiteboard. Then, draw it clean. This is like how God cleans away our sins when we ask for forgiveness. Think about someone you might need to forgive today.

PRAYER

Forgiving God, thank You for the gift of forgiveness. Thank You for Jesus, who made it possible. Help me to ask for forgiveness when I need it and to forgive others too. Amen.

Chapter 36: God's Mercy

"The Lord is good to all; he has compassion on all he has made." - Psalm 145:9

Mercy is when someone deserves punishment, but instead, they receive kindness and compassion. God shows us incredible mercy. We all make mistakes and fall short of God's perfect ways. We deserve consequences for our wrong choices. God, in His great love, chooses to show us mercy instead. He offers us a way back to Him through Jesus, instead of giving us what our sin deserves. This is a wonderful gift.

 ACTIVITY

Think about a time when someone was kind to you even when you made a mistake. How did that make you feel? Draw a picture of a helping hand, showing how God extends His mercy to us.

PRAYER

Merciful God, thank You for showing me kindness and not giving me what my sins deserve. Help me to be merciful to others, just as You are merciful to me. Amen.

Chapter 37: God's Faithfulness

"Know therefore that the Lord your God is God; he is the faithful God, keeping his covenant of love to a thousand generations of those who love him and keep his commands." - Deuteronomy 7:9

God is faithful, which means He always keeps His promises. He never changes His mind, and He never fails. From the beginning of creation, God has shown His faithfulness. He promised a Savior, and He sent Jesus. He promises to be with us, and He is. We can rely completely on God because He is always true to His word. His faithfulness gives us a strong foundation for our lives.

 ACTIVITY

Think about a time someone kept a promise to you. How did that make you feel? Write down one promise God has made in the Bible that you remember.

PRAYER

Faithful God, thank You for always keeping Your promises. Help me to trust in Your faithfulness every day. Amen.

Chapter 38: God's Peace

"I have told you these things, so that in me you may have peace. In this world you will have trouble. But take heart! I have overcome the world." - *John 16:33*

The world can sometimes feel busy or even scary. God offers us a special kind of peace, a peace that comes from knowing Him. This peace is not just about everything being quiet around us. It is a deep calm in our hearts, knowing that God is in control and He cares for us. When we trust God, His peace can fill our hearts, even when things are difficult.

 **ACTIVITY**

Find a quiet place and take a few slow, deep breaths. Imagine God's peace filling your heart. Draw a calm scene, like a still lake or a quiet forest.

PRAYER

God of Peace, thank You for the peace You offer. Help me to trust You with my worries and to find Your peace in my heart. Amen.

Chapter 39: God's Joy

"But let all who take refuge in you be glad; let them ever sing for joy. Spread your protection over them, that those who love your name may rejoice in you.." - Psalm 5:11

Joy is more than just being happy for a moment. It is a deep, lasting happiness that comes from knowing God and being close to Him. We can have joy even when things are not perfect, because our joy comes from God, who is always good. God delights in us, and He wants us to experience true joy in Him. His joy gives us strength.

 **ACTIVITY**

Think about something that brings you true joy. How does it make you feel inside? Write down three things that make you joyful about God.

PRAYER

Joyful God, thank You for filling my heart with Your joy. Help me to find my strength and happiness in You always. Amen.

Chapter 40: God's Great Love

"For God so loved the world that he gave his one and only Son, that whoever believes in him shall not perish but have eternal life." - John 3:16

We have spent forty days learning about God as our amazing Creator. We have seen His power, wisdom, goodness, holiness, presence, and faithfulness. All these qualities are wrapped up in His greatest attribute: His love. God's love is immense and never-ending. He loved us so much that He created us, and He loves us so much that He made a way for us to be close to Him, even after sin entered the world. His love is the most important truth of all.

 **ACTIVITY**

Draw a large heart. Inside the heart, write words or draw pictures that remind you of God's great love for you (e.g., family, friends, nature, Jesus).

PRAYER

Loving God, thank You for Your great, never-ending love. Thank You for creating me and for all the ways You show Your love every day. Help me to love You back with all my heart. Amen.

Chapter 41: Noah and the Flood

"The Lord saw how great the wickedness of the human race had become on the earth, and that every inclination of the thoughts of the human heart was only evil all the time. The Lord regretted that he had made human beings on the earth, and his heart was deeply troubled. But Noah found favor in the eyes of the Lord." - Genesis 6:5-6, 8

As generations multiplied after Adam and Eve, human corruption spread. Violence filled the land, and God, grieving over such deep-rooted wickedness, announced a decisive judgment: a global flood that would bring an end to all flesh.

Amid the darkness stood one man: Noah, who "walked faithfully with God." Because of this relationship, Noah and his family were chosen to enter the ark and survive. The coming flood highlighted both sides of God's character: His holiness, which cannot ignore persistent sin, and His mercy, which preserves those who trust Him and live uprightly.

 **ACTIVITY**

Think about a time you saw something that made you sad because it was wrong. What did you wish would happen? Draw a picture of a single person standing tall in a crowd, representing Noah standing out for God.

PRAYER

Holy God, I am sorry for the bad things people do. Thank You for seeing those who love You, like Noah. Help me to always choose to do what is right in Your eyes. Amen.

Chapter 42: Building the Ark

"So Noah did everything just as God commanded him." - Genesis 6:22

God told Noah to build a very large boat called an ark. This was not a small rowboat. It was huge, like a giant box, and God gave Noah exact instructions on how to build it and what materials to use. Noah had never seen rain before, let alone a flood like God described. Building an ark on dry land must have seemed strange to others. Noah trusted God completely. He obeyed every single instruction God gave him. This shows Noah's great faith and obedience.

 ## ACTIVITY

Imagine God asked you to build something very unusual. Would you trust Him and follow His directions? Try to build a small boat out of paper or blocks. Think about how much work Noah put into building the ark.

 ## PRAYER

Obedient God, thank You for Noah's example of faith. Help me to trust and obey You completely, even when Your instructions seem big or unusual. Amen.

Chapter 43: God's Promise to Noah

"But I will establish my covenant with you, and you will enter the ark—you and your sons and your wife and your sons' wives with you." - *Genesis 6:18*

As Noah worked on the ark, God made a special promise to him. God promised to establish His covenant (which is an unbreakable promise) with Noah. This meant God would save Noah, his family, and animals from the flood. God kept His promise. He brought the animals to Noah, and they all went into the ark. God always keeps His promises, and we can rely on His word.

 **ACTIVITY**

Think about a promise someone made to you that made you feel safe or happy. How did it feel when they kept it? Write down one animal you would have liked to see go into the ark.

PRAYER

Promise-Keeping God, thank You for always keeping Your promises. Thank You for saving Noah and his family. Help me to remember that Your promises are true. Amen.

Chapter 44: The Rainbow Covenant

"I have set my rainbow in the clouds, and it will be the sign of the covenant between me and the earth." - Genesis 9:13

The rain came, and the flood covered the earth, just as God said. Noah, his family, and all the animals were safe inside the ark. After many days, the waters went down, and the ark rested on a mountain. When Noah and his family came out, God made another promise. He promised He would never again destroy all life on earth with a flood. As a sign of this promise, God put a beautiful rainbow in the sky. The rainbow is specifically a symbol of the promise to not destroy the Earth by flood again.

 ## ACTIVITY

Look for a rainbow after it rains, or draw one if you cannot see one. Think about how the rainbow is a beautiful reminder of God's promise. What colors are in your rainbow?

 ## PRAYER

Faithful God, thank You for the beautiful rainbow and for Your promise never to flood the whole earth again. Help me to remember Your faithfulness whenever I see a rainbow. Amen.

Chapter 45: Listening to God

"My sheep listen to my voice; I know them, and they follow me." - John 10:27

Noah's story teaches us how important it is to listen to God. Noah heard God's instructions, and he obeyed them, even when they seemed difficult or unusual. Because he listened and obeyed, Noah and his family were saved. God still speaks to us today through the Bible, through prayer, and sometimes through wise people. When we listen to God, we can trust that He will guide us and keep us safe.

 **ACTIVITY**

Play a game where one person gives instructions, and the other person has to listen carefully and follow them exactly. How well did you listen? Think about how important it is to listen to God's voice.

PRAYER

Listening God, help me to listen carefully to Your voice. Guide me through Your Word and help me to obey all that You ask me to do. Amen.

Chapter 46: Abraham's Call

"The Lord had said to Abram, 'Go from your country, your people and your father's household to the land I will show you.'" - Genesis 12:1

Many years after Noah, God spoke to a man named Abram, who lived in a city called Ur. God told Abram to leave his home, his relatives, and everything he knew, and go to a land God would show him. This was a big step of faith! Abram did not know where he was going, but he trusted God. He packed up his family and possessions and began his journey. This shows Abram's willingness to obey God, even when the path was unclear.

 **ACTIVITY**

Imagine moving to a brand new place where you know no one. How would you feel? Draw a simple map showing a path from one place to another, thinking about Abram's journey of faith.

PRAYER

Guiding God, thank You for leading us. Help me to trust You and follow Your call, even when I do not know what the future holds. Amen.

Chapter 47: God's Promises to Abraham

"I will make you into a great nation, and I will bless you; I will make your name great, and you will be a blessing." - Genesis 12:2

As Abram obeyed, God made him some amazing promises. God promised to make Abram into a great nation, to bless him, and to make his name great. God also promised that through Abram, all the families on earth would be blessed.

Most importantly, God promised Abram a son, even though Abram and his wife, Sarai, were very old and had no children. God later changed Abram's name to Abraham, meaning "father of many nations." These promises show God's incredible power to do the impossible and His faithfulness to His word.

 **ACTIVITY**

Think about a big dream you have for your future. How does it feel to think about it coming true? Write down one of God's promises to Abraham that you find amazing.

PRAYER

Promise-Keeping God, thank You for Your amazing promises to Abraham. Help me to believe that You can do anything, and that Your promises are true for me too. Amen.

Chapter 48: Abraham and Lot

"Then Abram said to Lot, 'Let's not have any quarreling between you and me, or between your herders and mine, for we are close relatives. Is not the whole land before you? Let's part company. If you go to the left, I'll go to the right; or if you go to the right, I'll go to the left.'" - Genesis 13:8-9

Abraham traveled with his nephew, Lot. They both had many animals and possessions, so much that the land could not support them living together. There was arguing between their herdsmen. Abraham, being a man of peace and generosity, gave Lot the first choice of land. Lot chose the well-watered plains, which seemed like the best choice.

Abraham let Lot go first, trusting God to provide for him. This shows Abraham's selfless spirit and his faith that God would take care of him no matter what.

ACTIVITY

Think about a time you had to share something or let someone else choose first. Was it easy or hard? Draw two paths separating, representing Abraham and Lot parting ways.

PRAYER

Generous God, help me to be selfless and peaceful like Abraham. Help me to trust that You will always provide for me. Amen.

Chapter 49: Trusting God for a Child

"Is anything too hard for the Lord? I will return to you at the appointed time next year, and Sarah will have a son." - Genesis 18:14

God had promised Abraham (Abram's new name) and Sarah (Sarai's new name) a son, but many years passed, and they were still childless. They were very old. It seemed impossible for them to have a baby. Sarah even laughed when she heard the promise again. God reminded them that nothing is too hard for Him. This was a test of their faith. They had to learn to trust God's timing and His power to do what seemed impossible.

 **ACTIVITY**

Think about something you have been waiting for a long time. How does it feel to wait? Draw a picture of a tiny seed, representing a promise that will grow.

PRAYER

Patient God, thank You for Your promises. Help me to trust Your timing and believe that nothing is too hard for You. Amen.

Chapter 50: Isaac Is Born

"Now the Lord was gracious to Sarah as he had said, and the Lord did for Sarah what he had promised. Sarah became pregnant and bore a son to Abraham in his old age, at the very time God had promised him." - Genesis 21:1-2

Just as God promised, when Abraham was 100 years old and Sarah was 90, Sarah gave birth to a son! They named him Isaac, which means "he laughs," because Sarah had laughed when she first heard God's promise. Isaac's birth was a miracle. It proved that God always keeps His word, even when it seems impossible from a human point of view. God's power is greater than any obstacle.

 **ACTIVITY**

Think about a time you were surprised and happy because something amazing happened. How did that feel? Draw a picture of a baby, representing the miracle of Isaac's birth.

PRAYER

Miracle-Working God, thank You for keeping Your promises and doing amazing things. Help me to remember that You are a God of miracles. Amen.

Chapter 51: A Test of Faith

"Then God said, 'Take your son, your only son, whom you love—Isaac—and go to the region of Moriah. Sacrifice him there as a burnt offering on a mountain I will show you.'" - Genesis 22:2

After years of waiting for the son God had promised, Abraham now faced the unthinkable: give that very son back as a sacrifice. At dawn he saddled a donkey, split the wood himself, and set out on a three-day trek to the mountains of Moriah. With every step, the weight of the wood on Isaac's shoulders mirrored the weight in Abraham's heart.

Abraham moved forward because he believed the God who had given life to a barren womb could also give life back to a slain son. When Isaac asked, "Where is the lamb for the sacrifice?" Abraham answered, "God Himself will provide."

Obedience did not erase his grief, but it did express his unwavering confidence in God's faithfulness: a trust strong enough to follow even the hardest command.

 # ACTIVITY

Think about a time you were asked to do something very hard that you did not understand. How did you feel? Draw a picture of a path leading up a mountain, representing Abraham's journey of faith.

PRAYER

Trustworthy God, sometimes Your plans are hard to understand. Help me to trust You completely, even when things are difficult, just like Abraham did. Amen.

Chapter 52: God Provides

"Abraham looked up and there in a thicket he saw a ram[a] caught by its horns. He went over and took the ram and sacrificed it as a burnt offering instead of his son. 14 So Abraham called that place The Lord Will Provide. And to this day it is said, "On the mountain of the Lord it will be provided." - Genesis 22:13-14

Abraham and Isaac went to the mountain. Isaac asked where the lamb for the sacrifice was. Abraham replied that God Himself would provide the lamb. Just as Abraham was about to obey God's command, an angel of the Lord called out from heaven and stopped him. God saw Abraham's faith. Nearby, a ram was caught in a bush, and God provided it as the sacrifice instead of Isaac. This story shows that God provides in line with His purposes, not always in the exact way we want.

 **ACTIVITY**

Think about a time you needed something, and it was provided just when you needed it most. How did that make you feel? Write down one thing God has provided for you recently.

PRAYER

Providing God, thank You for always meeting my needs. Help me to remember that You are "The Lord Will Provide" in every situation. Amen.

Chapter 53: Rebekah and Isaac

"Then Rebekah got up with her attendants and rode on the camels and went with the man. So the servant took Rebekah and departed." - Genesis 24:61

Abraham wanted Isaac to marry someone who also loved God. He sent his servant to his homeland to find a wife for Isaac. The servant prayed for God's guidance. God led him to Rebekah, a kind and helpful woman. She offered water to the servant and his camels, showing her good heart. Rebekah chose to go with the servant and became Isaac's wife. This shows how God guides us in important decisions when we seek His will and how He brings people together.

 ACTIVITY

Think about a time you helped someone without being asked. How did it feel to be helpful? Draw a picture of two people shaking hands, representing a new friendship or relationship.

PRAYER

Guiding God, thank You for leading us in our lives. Help me to be kind and helpful to others, and to trust Your guidance in all my choices. Amen.

Chapter 54: Jacob and Esau

"Then Jacob gave Esau some bread and some lentil stew. He ate and drank, and then got up and left. So Esau despised his birthright." - Genesis 25:34

Isaac and Rebekah's twin sons could not have been more different. Esau, the firstborn, roamed the fields as a skilled hunter, while Jacob preferred life around the tents, tending flocks and cooking stews. By custom the elder son received the birthright, a double share of the inheritance and the family's covenant blessing.

Esau treated that privilege lightly, trading it to Jacob for a single meal when hunger clouded his judgment.

Years later, as Isaac's eyesight faded, Rebekah was determined to secure the covenant blessing for the son God had chosen.

She coached Jacob through a risky deception: covering his arms with goatskins, dressing him in Esau's clothes, and serving Isaac a dish that tasted like Esau's game. Isaac, convinced, bestowed the blessing on Jacob instead of Esau.

The scheme succeeded, but it shattered the brothers' relationship and sent Jacob fleeing for his life. The episode reminds us that human choices, even flawed ones, can't derail God's larger plan. Despite family favoritism, deceit, and conflict, God still shaped Jacob into "Israel," father of the twelve tribes. The story urges us to weigh our decisions carefully, knowing they carry real consequences, while trusting that God's purposes remain steady even when our paths twist and tangle.

 **ACTIVITY**

Think about a time you wanted something badly and were tempted to get it in a wrong way. What did you do? Draw two different paths, one straight and one winding, representing different choices.

PRAYER

God, help me to be honest and fair in all my dealings. Help me to avoid trickery and to trust Your way of doing things. Amen.

Chapter 55: Jacob's Dream

"He had a dream in which he saw a stairway resting on the earth, with its top reaching to heaven, and the angels of God were ascending and descending on it. There above it stood the Lord, and he said: "I am the Lord, the God of your father Abraham and the God of Isaac. I will give you and your descendants the land on which you are lying.." - Genesis 28:12-13

After Jacob tricked Esau, he had to run away from home. One night, while sleeping with a stone for a pillow, Jacob had an amazing dream. He saw a stairway reaching from earth to heaven, with angels going up and down on it. God stood at the top and spoke to Jacob, renewing the promises He had made to Abraham and Isaac. God promised to be with Jacob, protect him, and bring him back to his homeland. This dream showed Jacob that God was with him, even when he was alone and far from home.

 # ACTIVITY

Imagine you are having a wonderful dream. What would you see? Draw a simple ladder or stairway reaching up to the sky, symbolizing God's connection to us.

PRAYER

God, thank You for being with me wherever I go. Thank You for Your promises to protect and guide me. Help me to feel Your presence, even when I am alone. Amen.

Chapter 56: Jacob Works for Laban

"So Jacob served seven years for Rachel, and they seemed to him but a few days because of his love for her." - Genesis 29:20

Jacob traveled to his uncle Laban's house. There, he fell in love with Laban's daughter, Rachel. Laban agreed to let Jacob marry Rachel if he worked for him for seven years. Jacob worked hard, and the seven years felt like only a few days because he loved Rachel so much. But Laban tricked Jacob and gave him Leah, Rachel's older sister, instead. Jacob then worked another seven years for Rachel. This shows that even when people are unfair to us, God can still use those situations and teach us patience and perseverance.

 **ACTIVITY**

Think about a time you worked hard for something you really wanted. How did it feel to finally achieve it? Draw a picture of a person working hard, like planting seeds or building something.

PRAYER

Patient God, help me to work hard and to be patient when things do not go as planned. Thank You for being with me even when others are unfair. Amen.

Chapter 57: Jacob Wrestles with God

"Then the man said, 'Your name will no longer be Jacob, but Israel, because you have struggled with God and with humans and have overcome.'" - Genesis 32:28

Many years later, Jacob decided to return home and face Esau. He was very afraid. One night, Jacob was alone, and a mysterious man wrestled with him until daybreak. Jacob would not let go until the man blessed him. The man touched Jacob's hip, injuring him, and then blessed him, changing his name from Jacob to Israel, which means "he struggles with God." This powerful encounter showed Jacob that he had truly wrestled with God and had been blessed. It reminds us that sometimes we struggle with God, but He is always there, and He blesses us.

 **ACTIVITY**

Think about a time you had a big struggle or challenge. How did you get through it? Draw two stick figures wrestling, representing Jacob's struggle and perseverance.

PRAYER

Strong God, thank You for being with me even when I struggle. Help me to hold onto You and to learn from every challenge. Amen.

Chapter 58: Joseph's Dreams

"Then he had another dream, and he told it to his brothers. 'Listen,' he said, 'I had another dream, and this time the sun and moon and eleven stars were bowing down to me.'" - Genesis 37:9

Jacob, now called Israel, had twelve sons, but his affection for seventeen-year-old Joseph was obvious: he made Joseph a richly ornamented robe that announced favoritism every time the boy walked past.

Joseph then shared two startling dreams: in one, his brothers' sheaves of grain bowed to his; in the other, the sun, moon, and eleven stars did the same. To most of the brothers, the dreams felt like arrogant predictions of supremacy, and their jealousy hardened into hatred. Reuben, the eldest, stood apart: although irritated, he felt responsible for Joseph's safety and later tried to steer his brothers away from violence.

These early rifts set in motion a chain of events, betrayal, slavery, and eventually salvation, through which God would move the family to Egypt and unfold His larger covenant plan. The episode reminds us that unchecked envy breeds conflict, yet even our tangled family struggles can become threads in the tapestry of God's faithful purposes.

 **ACTIVITY**

Think about a dream you have had. Was it a happy dream or a strange one? Draw a simple picture of stars and a sun, representing Joseph's dreams.

PRAYER

God, thank You for giving us dreams and for having a plan for our lives. Help me to trust Your plan, even when it is hard to understand. Amen.

Chapter 59: Joseph Is Sold

"So when the Midianite merchants came by, his brothers pulled Joseph up out of the pit and sold him for twenty shekels of silver to the Ishmaelites, who took him to Egypt." - Genesis 37:28

Joseph's brothers were so jealous and angry about his dreams and their father's love for him that they decided to get rid of him. They first planned to kill him, but Reuben stopped them. Instead, they threw him into a pit. Then, when a group of traders came by, they sold Joseph as a slave for twenty pieces of silver. They told their father that a wild animal had killed Joseph. This was a terrible, cruel act. It shows how jealousy and hatred can lead to very bad choices.

 # ACTIVITY

Think about a time you felt jealous or angry with someone. What happened? How did you deal with those feelings? Write down one way you can show kindness to a sibling or friend today.

PRAYER

God, help me to overcome feelings of jealousy and anger. Help me to be kind and loving to my family and friends, even when I disagree with them. Amen.

Chapter 60: Joseph in Potiphar's House

"The Lord was with Joseph so that he prospered, and he lived in the house of his Egyptian master. When his master saw that the Lord was with him and that the Lord gave him success in everything he did, he put him in charge of his household, and he entrusted to his care everything he owned." - Genesis 39:2-4

Joseph was taken to Egypt and sold to a man named Potiphar, who was an officer for Pharaoh, the king of Egypt. Even though Joseph was a slave, God was with him. Everything Joseph did succeeded because God blessed him. Potiphar saw this and put Joseph in charge of his entire household. Joseph was honest and hardworking. This shows that even in very difficult circumstances, God can be with us and help us to do well.

 **ACTIVITY**

Think about a time you had to do a chore or a task you did not enjoy. How did you do it? Draw a simple house, representing Potiphar's household, and a small figure diligently working inside.

PRAYER

God, thank You for being with me even when things are hard. Help me to be hardworking and honest in everything I do, knowing You are always with me. Amen.

Chapter 61: Joseph in Prison

"But while Joseph was there in the prison, the Lord was with him; he showed him kindness and granted him favor in the eyes of the prison warden." - Genesis 39:20-21

Joseph was doing very well in Potiphar's house. However, Potiphar's wife told a lie about Joseph, and because of this lie, Joseph was thrown into prison. This was very unfair! Joseph had done nothing wrong. Even in prison, God was with Joseph. The prison warden saw that Joseph was trustworthy and put him in charge of all the other prisoners. This shows that even when we face unfairness or difficult situations, God is still with us, and He can open doors for us.

 **ACTIVITY**

Think about a time you were blamed for something you did not do. How did it feel? Draw a key, representing how God can open doors even in tough situations.

PRAYER

God, thank You for being with me when things are unfair. Help me to trust You and to be patient, knowing You are always working for my good. Amen.

Chapter 62: Interpreting Dreams

"We both had dreams," they answered, "but there is no one to interpret them." Then Joseph said to them, "Do not interpretations belong to God? Tell me your dreams." - Genesis 40:8

While Joseph was in prison, two of Pharaoh's officials, the cupbearer and the baker, were also put in prison. Each of them had a strange dream one night. They were confused and did not know what their dreams meant. Joseph told them that God is the One who gives dreams and understands their meaning. Joseph, with God's help, was able to interpret their dreams. This showed that God was working through Joseph, even in a dark prison.

 **ACTIVITY**

Think about a dream you have had. Was it clear or confusing? Draw a simple thought bubble with a question mark inside, representing a confusing dream.

PRAYER

Wise God, thank You for giving us understanding. Help me to remember that all wisdom comes from You, and You can help me understand difficult things. Amen.

Chapter 63: Pharaoh's Dreams

"So Pharaoh sent for Joseph, and he was quickly brought from the dungeon. When he had shaved and changed his clothes, he came before Pharaoh." - Genesis 41:14

Joseph correctly interpreted the dreams of the cupbearer and the baker. The cupbearer was restored to his position, and the baker was executed, just as Joseph said. Two years later, Pharaoh, the king of Egypt, had two disturbing dreams that no one in his kingdom could interpret. Pharaoh's cupbearer finally remembered Joseph in prison and told Pharaoh about him. Pharaoh sent for Joseph. This shows that God's timing is perfect. He waited for the right moment to bring Joseph out of prison and into a position where he could help many people.

 **ACTIVITY**

Think about a time you had to wait for something important. Was it hard to wait? Draw a clock with a happy face, representing God's perfect timing.

PRAYER

God of perfect timing, thank You for working things out in Your way. Help me to be patient and to trust Your timing in my life. Amen.

Chapter 64: Joseph Becomes Governor

"So Pharaoh said to Joseph, 'Since God has made all this known to you, there is no one so discerning and wise as you. You shall be in charge of my palace, and all my people are to submit to your orders. Only with respect to the throne will I be greater than you.'" - Genesis 41:39-40

Joseph stood before Pharaoh and, with God's help, interpreted Pharaoh's dreams. The dreams meant there would be seven years of plenty, followed by seven years of severe famine across the land. Joseph also gave Pharaoh wise advice on how to prepare for the famine.

Pharaoh was so impressed by Joseph's wisdom and by the fact that God was with him, that he made Joseph the second-most powerful person in all of Egypt, the governor! Joseph went from being a prisoner to a powerful leader in one day. This shows God's amazing ability to change situations and use people for His purposes.

 **ACTIVITY**

Imagine you suddenly got a very important job. How would you feel? Draw a picture of a crown or a scepter, symbolizing leadership and authority.

PRAYER

Powerful God, thank You for Your wisdom and for placing people in positions where they can serve You. Help me to be wise and to use any influence I have for good. Amen.

Chapter 65: The Famine Begins

"When the famine had spread over all the country, Joseph opened all the storehouses and sold grain to the Egyptians, for the famine was severe throughout Egypt." - Genesis 41:56

Just as Joseph had interpreted, the seven years of plenty came, and Egypt gathered huge amounts of grain. Then, the seven years of famine began. The famine was severe, not only in Egypt but also in all the surrounding countries. People were hungry and desperate. Joseph, as governor, opened the storehouses and sold grain to the people, saving many lives. This shows God's foresight and how He used Joseph to protect and provide for many people during a very difficult time.

 **ACTIVITY**

Think about a time you were very hungry. How did it feel to finally eat? Draw a picture of a full basket of food, representing God's provision.

PRAYER

Providing God, thank You for always taking care of us and for giving us what we need. Help me to be grateful for my food and to remember those who are hungry. Amen.

Chapter 66: Joseph's Brothers Come to Egypt

"Now Joseph was the governor of the land, the person who sold grain to all its people. So when Joseph's brothers arrived, they bowed down to him with their faces to the ground.." - Genesis 42:6

The famine was so severe that Jacob (Joseph's father) sent his ten older sons to Egypt to buy grain. They did not know that Joseph was the powerful governor. When they arrived, they bowed down before Joseph, just as his dreams had foretold many years earlier. Joseph recognized them, but they did not recognize him. This was a surprising moment, as God's plan continued to unfold in unexpected ways.

 **ACTIVITY**

Imagine meeting someone you knew a long time ago, but they have changed so much you do not recognize them. How would that feel? Draw a simple picture of people bowing, representing respect.

PRAYER

God, thank You for working in mysterious ways to bring about Your plans. Help me to see Your hand in unexpected situations. Amen.

Chapter 67: Joseph Tests His Brothers

"This is how you will be tested: As surely as Pharaoh lives, you will not leave this place unless your youngest brother comes here." - Genesis 42:15

Joseph did not immediately tell his brothers who he was. Instead, he tested them to see if their hearts had changed. He accused them of being spies and put them in prison for three days. He then told them they must bring their youngest brother, Benjamin, back to Egypt to prove their story. This was a difficult test, but Joseph wanted to see if they were still the same cruel brothers who had sold him into slavery. This shows Joseph's wisdom in testing their character.

 **ACTIVITY**

Think about a time you had to prove something to someone. How did you do it? Draw a simple scale, representing a test of fairness or truth.

PRAYER

Wise God, help me to understand people's hearts and to make good judgments. Help me to learn from my mistakes and to grow in character. Amen.

Chapter 68: Benjamin Comes to Egypt

"Then Judah said to his father Israel, 'Send the boy along with me so that we may go at once, and live and not die—we and you and our children.'" - *Genesis 43:8*

The famine continued to be severe, and Jacob's family ran out of food again. They had to return to Egypt for more grain. Jacob was very hesitant to let Benjamin go, as he was the only remaining son of Rachel. Judah, one of Joseph's brothers, promised to take responsibility for Benjamin's safety. Finally, Jacob agreed, and they took Benjamin to Egypt. This shows Judah's changed heart and his willingness to protect his younger brother, a big difference from how they treated Joseph years ago.

 **ACTIVITY**

Think about a time you stood up for someone or took responsibility for them. How did that feel? Draw a picture of two hands holding each other, symbolizing support and responsibility.

PRAYER

God, help me to be responsible and to protect those who are weaker or in need. Thank You for changing hearts and bringing families together. Amen.

Chapter 69: The Silver Cup

"Then he ordered the steward of his house, 'Fill the men's sacks with as much food as they can carry, and put each man's silver in the mouth of his sack. Then put my silver cup in the mouth of the youngest one's sack, along with the silver for his grain.'" - Genesis 44:1-2

When Joseph's brothers returned to Egypt with Benjamin, Joseph invited them to a feast. He treated Benjamin with special favor. As they prepared to leave with their grain, Joseph secretly had his silver cup placed in Benjamin's sack. After they left, Joseph sent his steward to chase them and accuse them of stealing the cup. When the cup was found in Benjamin's sack, the brothers were heartbroken. This was another test from Joseph to see how his brothers would react to Benjamin being in trouble.

 **ACTIVITY**

Imagine you are accused of something you did not do. How would you feel? Draw a picture of a hidden object, representing the silver cup.

PRAYER

God, help me to be honest and to stand up for what is right, even when it is difficult. Guide me when I am tested. Amen.

Chapter 70: Joseph Reveals Himself

"Then Joseph could no longer control himself before all his attendants, and he cried out, "Have everyone leave my presence!" So there was no one with Joseph when he made himself known to his brothers. And he wept so loudly that the Egyptians heard him, and Pharaoh's household heard about it. Joseph said to his brothers, "I am Joseph! Is my father still living?" But his brothers were not able to answer him, because they were terrified at his presence.?"' - Genesis 45:1-3

When the silver cup was found, Judah stepped forward and pleaded with Joseph, offering himself as a slave in Benjamin's place. Judah showed great love and sacrifice for his younger brother. Seeing their changed hearts, Joseph could no longer hold back. He sent everyone else away and revealed himself to his brothers, weeping loudly. "I am Joseph!"

he cried. His brothers were terrified, but Joseph told them not to be afraid. This was a powerful moment of forgiveness and reconciliation. It shows how God can heal broken relationships.

 **ACTIVITY**

Think about a time you forgave someone or someone forgave you. How did that make you feel? Draw two figures hugging, representing forgiveness and reconciliation.

PRAYER

God of reconciliation, thank You for healing broken relationships and for the power of forgiveness. Help me to forgive others and to seek forgiveness when I need to. Amen.

Chapter 71: Family Reunited

"And you are to tell my father about all my glory in Egypt and about everything you have seen. And bring my father down here quickly." - Genesis 45:13

Joseph told his brothers that God had sent him to Egypt to save many lives, including their family's. He told them to go back to Canaan quickly and bring their father, Jacob, and all their families to Egypt. Joseph promised to provide for them during the remaining years of famine. The brothers rushed back with the good news. Jacob was overjoyed to hear that Joseph was alive. This was a wonderful reunion, showing God's kindness in bringing a family back together after so many years of separation and pain.

 **ACTIVITY**

Think about a time you were reunited with someone you missed very much. How did that feel? Draw a picture of a happy family gathering, representing Jacob's family coming together.

PRAYER

God of reunions, thank You for bringing families together and for healing brokenness. Help me to cherish my family and to seek reconciliation when needed. Amen.

Chapter 72: God's Good Plan

"You intended to harm me, but God intended it for good to accomplish what is now being done, the saving of many lives." - Genesis 50:20

Joseph explained to his brothers that even though they meant to harm him by selling him into slavery, God had a good plan. God used their evil actions to save many people from the famine, including their own family. This amazing truth shows that God can take bad situations and turn them into something good. He is always working, even when we cannot see His hand, to fulfill His good purposes. We can trust His overall plan.

 **ACTIVITY**

Think about a time something bad happened, but something good came out of it later. How did that make you feel? Write down one way God has turned a difficult situation into something good in your life or someone you know.

PRAYER

God of good plans, thank You for working all things for good. Help me to trust that You are always in control, even when things seem bad. Amen.

Chapter 73: Living in Egypt

"So Israel [Jacob] settled in Egypt in the land of Goshen. They acquired property there and were fruitful and increased greatly in number." - Genesis 47:27

Jacob and his entire family, including all his children, grandchildren, and their families, moved to Egypt. Joseph settled them in the best part of the land, Goshen, where there was good pasture for their animals. They lived there for many years and grew into a large nation, just as God had promised Abraham. This period in Egypt was a time of growth and safety for God's chosen people, all because of Joseph's position and God's faithfulness.

 # ACTIVITY

Imagine moving to a new country. What would be exciting? What would be challenging? Draw a picture of a family growing larger, representing Jacob's family in Egypt.

PRAYER

Providing God, thank You for always taking care of Your people. Help me to be thankful for the safe places You provide for me. Amen.

Chapter 74: God's Care for His People

"The Lord watches over all who love him, but all the wicked he will destroy." - Psalm 145:20

The story of Joseph reminds us that God always cares for His people. He was with Joseph through all his hardships: being sold into slavery, being falsely accused, and being forgotten in prison. God never left Joseph. God also cared for Joseph's family by sending Joseph ahead to Egypt to save them from the famine. God's care is constant and personal. He watches over us and works behind the scenes to protect and provide for us.

 # ACTIVITY

Think about a time you felt God's care for you. What happened?
Write down one way God has shown He cares for you recently.

_____

_____

_____

_____

_____

_____

_____

_____

_____

PRAYER

Caring God, thank You for always watching over me and caring for
me. Help me to feel Your presence and Your love every day. Amen.

Chapter 75: God's Timing Is Perfect

"There is a time for everything, and a season for every activity under the heavens." - Ecclesiastes 3:1

Joseph spent many years as a slave and then in prison before God raised him up to be governor of Egypt. It must have felt like a very long time to Joseph. God's timing is always perfect. He waited until the exact right moment to bring Joseph out of prison, when Pharaoh needed someone to interpret his dreams and save Egypt from famine. God knows the best time for everything. We can trust His timing, even when we have to wait.

 **ACTIVITY**

Think about a time you had to wait for something important, and it turned out to be worth the wait. How did that feel? Draw a clock with the hands pointing to a specific, important moment.

PRAYER

God of perfect timing, thank You for knowing the best time for everything. Help me to be patient and to trust Your timing in my life. Amen.

Chapter 76: Learning from Mistakes

"Whoever conceals their sins does not prosper, but the one who confesses and renounces them finds mercy." - Proverbs 28:13

Joseph's brothers made a terrible mistake when they sold him into slavery. This caused many years of pain and separation. However, through the years of famine and their interactions with Joseph in Egypt, they learned important lessons about their actions. They showed remorse and a changed heart, especially Judah. God can use our mistakes and the consequences that follow to teach us and help us grow. It is important to learn from our errors and seek to do better.

 **ACTIVITY**

Think about a mistake you made. What did you learn from it? Write down one lesson you learned from Joseph's brothers' story.

_____

_____

_____

_____

_____

_____

_____

_____

_____

_____

PRAYER

God, help me to learn from my mistakes and to turn away from wrong choices. Thank You for Your mercy when I confess my sins. Amen.

Chapter 77: Forgiving Others

"Bear with each other and forgive one another if any of you has a grievance against someone. Forgive as the Lord forgave you." - Colossians 3:13

Joseph had every reason to be angry and bitter towards his brothers for what they did to him. They caused him so much suffering. Joseph chose to forgive them. He understood that God had used their bad actions for a good purpose. Forgiveness does not mean forgetting what happened, but it means letting go of anger and choosing to show kindness. Forgiving others can bring healing and peace to everyone involved.

 **ACTIVITY**

Think about someone you need to forgive, or a time someone forgave you. How did that feel? Draw a picture of a broken heart being mended, representing the healing power of forgiveness.

PRAYER

Forgiving God, thank You for showing me how to forgive. Help me to forgive those who have hurt me, just as You forgive me. Amen.

Chapter 78: Being Patient

"But if we hope for what we do not yet have, we wait for it patiently." -
Romans 8:25

Joseph's story is a great example of patience. He was patient in slavery,
patient in prison, and patient as he waited for God's plan to unfold. He
did not give up hope or lose faith. Patience means waiting calmly and
trusting God's timing, even when things are difficult or take a long time. It
is a valuable quality that helps us grow stronger in our faith.

 **ACTIVITY**

Think about something you are waiting for right now. What helps you to be patient? Draw a picture of a seed slowly growing into a plant, representing patience and growth.

PRAYER

Patient God, help me to be patient in waiting for Your plans. Help me to trust You and to grow stronger while I wait. Amen.

Chapter 79: God's Protection

"The Lord is my strength and my shield; my heart trusts in him, and he helps me. My heart leaps for joy, and with my song I praise him." - Psalm 28:7

Throughout Joseph's life, even in the darkest times, God protected him. God protected him from his brothers' initial plan to kill him. He protected him in Potiphar's house and in prison. God's protection is not always about keeping bad things from happening, but it is about being with us through them and using them for His good purposes. We can trust that God is our shield and our defender.

 **ACTIVITY**

Think about a time you felt safe or protected. What made you feel that way? Draw a simple shield, representing God's protection over you.

PRAYER

Protecting God, thank You for being my shield and my strength. Help me to feel safe and secure in Your care always. Amen.

Chapter 80: God's Guidance

"I will instruct you and teach you in the way you should go; I will counsel you with my loving eye on you." - Psalm 32:8

Joseph's life was full of twists and turns, but God guided him every step of the way. God gave him dreams, gave him wisdom to interpret dreams, and put him in the right place at the right time. God's guidance helps us know what to do and where to go. We can ask God for guidance in our daily lives, and He promises to show us the way. His guidance leads us on the best path.

 **ACTIVITY**

Think about a time you needed help finding your way, like using a map or following directions. How did it feel to be guided? Draw a compass, representing God's guidance in our lives.

PRAYER

Guiding God, thank You for leading me. Help me to listen for Your instructions and to follow Your path each day. Amen.

Chapter 81: God's Provision

"And my God will meet all your needs according to the riches of his glory in Christ Jesus." - Philippians 4:19

Joseph's story is a powerful reminder of God's provision. God provided for Joseph in slavery and in prison. He provided wisdom to interpret dreams. He provided for Egypt and for Jacob's family during the famine. God always provides what we need, sometimes in surprising ways. We can trust Him to meet our needs, whether it is food, shelter, or strength for a difficult day.

 **ACTIVITY**

Think about something God has provided for you recently, big or small. Write it down. Draw a cornucopia (a horn overflowing with fruit and vegetables), symbolizing abundant provision.

PRAYER

Providing God, thank You for always meeting my needs. Help me to be thankful for all Your provisions and to trust You for what I need tomorrow. Amen.

Chapter 82: God's Strength

"I can do all this through him who gives me strength." - Philippians 4:13

Joseph faced many challenges that would have made most people give up. He was sold, lied about, and imprisoned. Through it all, God gave him strength to endure. God's strength helps us when we feel weak or overwhelmed. We do not have to rely on our own power. We can lean on God's mighty strength to get through tough times and to do what is right.

 **ACTIVITY**

Think about a time you felt weak or tired, but you found the strength to keep going. Where did that strength come from? Draw a strong arm flexing, representing God's strength.

PRAYER

Strong God, thank You for being my strength when I am weak. Help me to rely on You and to find courage in Your power. Amen.

Chapter 83: God's Wisdom for Decisions

"If any of you lacks wisdom, you should ask God, who gives generously to all without finding fault, and it will be given to you." - James 1:5

Joseph needed great wisdom to interpret Pharaoh's dreams and to manage all of Egypt during the famine. God gave him that wisdom. When we face choices, big or small, we can ask God for wisdom. He promises to give it generously to those who ask in faith. God's wisdom helps us make good decisions that honor Him and benefit others.

 # ACTIVITY

Think about a decision you need to make soon. It could be about homework, friends, or an activity. Write down the decision. Ask God for wisdom as you think about it.

_____

_____

_____

_____

_____

_____

_____

_____

_____

_____

PRAYER

Wise God, thank You for offering me Your wisdom. Please guide me in my decisions today and help me to choose what is right in Your eyes. Amen.

Chapter 84: God's Comfort

"Praise be to the God and Father of our Lord Jesus Christ, the Father of compassion and the God of all comfort." - 2 Corinthians 1:3

Joseph experienced much sadness and loneliness during his years of suffering. God was always there to comfort him. God's comfort is like a warm hug for our hearts when we are hurting. He understands our pain and promises to be close to the brokenhearted. When we receive God's comfort, we can then share that comfort with others who are hurting.

 **ACTIVITY**

Think about a time you felt sad and someone comforted you. How did that help? Draw a soft blanket or a gentle hand, representing God's comfort.

PRAYER

Comforting God, thank You for being with me when I am sad. Please comfort my heart and help me to comfort others who need it. Amen.

Chapter 85: God's Deliverance

"The Lord is my rock, my fortress and my deliverer; my God is my rock, in whom I take refuge." - Psalm 18:2

Joseph was delivered from the pit, from slavery, and from prison. God delivered him from difficult situations and brought him to a place of honor. God is a deliverer. He can rescue us from danger, from fear, and from the power of sin. We can trust Him to deliver us from our troubles, in His perfect way and time.

 **ACTIVITY**

Think about a time you were in trouble and someone helped you get out of it. How did that feel? Draw a simple drawing of someone being pulled out of a hole or reaching for a helping hand.

PRAYER

Delivering God, thank You for rescuing me from trouble. You are my strong tower and my refuge. Help me to trust You as my deliverer. Amen.

Chapter 86: God's Promises Are True

"The Lord is not slow in keeping his promise, as some understand slowness. Instead he is patient with you, not wanting anyone to perish, but everyone to come to repentance." - 2 Peter 3:9

From the promise to Abraham about his descendants to Joseph's dreams coming true, the stories in the Bible show us that God's promises are always true. He never breaks His word. This gives us great confidence. We can read the Bible and know that everything God says will happen, will happen. We can build our lives on His faithful promises.

 **ACTIVITY**

Think about a promise you are holding onto from God's Word. Write it down. Draw a scroll or an open book, representing God's unchanging promises.

PRAYER

Faithful God, thank You that Your promises are always true. Help me to believe Your Word and to stand firm on Your promises. Amen.

Chapter 87: Waiting on God

"But those who hope in the Lord will renew their strength. They will soar on wings like eagles; they will run and not grow weary, they will walk and not be faint." - Isaiah 40:31

Joseph waited many years for God's plan to unfold. He waited patiently, even when it was hard. Waiting on God means trusting His timing and not trying to rush ahead of Him. It means continuing to obey Him and do our best, even when we do not see immediate results. Waiting on God helps us grow in patience and strengthens our faith.

 **ACTIVITY**

Find a small seed. Think about how it has to wait patiently to grow into a plant. Draw a picture of an eagle soaring, representing renewed strength while waiting on God.

PRAYER

Patient God, help me to wait on You with a hopeful heart. Renew my strength as I trust in Your perfect timing. Amen.

Chapter 88: Speaking Truth

"Therefore each of you must put off falsehood and speak truthfully to your neighbor, for we are all members of one body." - Ephesians 4:25

Joseph spoke the truth when he interpreted dreams, even when the truth was difficult. Later, when he revealed himself to his brothers, he spoke truth to them about God's good plan. Speaking truth is important, even when it is hard. God is a God of truth, and He wants us to be truthful in all our words and actions. Speaking truth builds trust and honors God.

 **ACTIVITY**

Think about a time it was hard to tell the truth. What happened? Write down one way you can practice speaking truth today, even in small things.

_____

_____

_____

_____

_____

_____

_____

_____

_____

_____

PRAYER

Truthful God, help me to always speak the truth in love. Guide my words so that they honor You and build up others. Amen.

Chapter 89: Honoring Our Parents

"Honor your father and your mother, so that you may live long in the land the Lord your God is giving you." - Exodus 20:12

Joseph deeply honored his father, Jacob. Even after all the years of separation, he sent for him and provided for him in Egypt. God commands us to honor our father and mother. This means respecting them, obeying them, and treating them with love and kindness. When we honor our parents, we show respect for the authority God has placed in our lives, and it brings blessings.

 ACTIVITY

Think about one way you can show honor to your parents today. Maybe it is by doing a chore without being asked, or by listening carefully when they speak. Do that one thing.

 PRAYER

God, thank You for my parents. Help me to honor and respect them in all that I do and say. Amen.

Chapter 90: Being Humble

"Humble yourselves, therefore, under God's mighty hand, that he may lift you up in due time." - 1 Peter 5:6

Joseph went from being a favored son to a slave, then a prisoner, and finally a powerful governor. Through all these changes, Joseph remained humble. He did not boast about his abilities. He always gave God the glory for his wisdom and success. Humility means not thinking too highly of ourselves, but recognizing that all our gifts and successes come from God. God blesses the humble.

 **ACTIVITY**

Think about something you are good at. How can you use that skill to help others without showing off? Draw a small figure bowing, representing humility before God.

PRAYER

Humble God, help me to be humble in all my achievements. Remind me that all good things come from You. Amen.

Chapter 91: Overcoming Challenges

"I have told you these things, so that in me you may have peace. In this world you will have trouble. But take heart! I have overcome the world." -John 16:33

Joseph faced many difficult challenges in his life. He was betrayed, falsely accused, and forgotten. He did not let these challenges defeat him. With God's help, he overcame each one. We all face challenges, big and small. Joseph's story reminds us that with God by our side, we can overcome anything. We can find strength and hope in Him, even when things seem impossible.

 **ACTIVITY**

Think about a challenge you are facing right now. What is one small step you can take to overcome it? Draw a mountain with a path leading to the top, symbolizing overcoming a challenge.

PRAYER

Overcoming God, thank You for helping me face challenges. Give me strength and courage to overcome difficulties with Your help. Amen.

Chapter 92: God's Steadfast Love

"The steadfast love of the Lord never ceases; his mercies never come to an end; they are new every morning; great is your faithfulness." - *Lamentations 3:22-23*

Through all of Joseph's ups and downs, God's steadfast love never left him. Steadfast love means a love that is firm, unchanging, and loyal. God's love for Joseph, and for us, is like that. It does not waver. It is always there, no matter what circumstances we face. This steadfast love is a constant source of comfort and security.

 **ACTIVITY**

Think about someone whose love for you is always steady and reliable. How does that make you feel? Draw a strong anchor, representing God's steadfast love.

PRAYER

Steadfast God, thank You for Your unchanging love. Help me to rest in Your love and to know that You are always with me. Amen.

Chapter 93: God's Greatness

"Great is the Lord and most worthy of praise; his greatness no one can fathom." - Psalm 145:3

The entire story of Joseph, from his dreams to his rise in Egypt and the saving of his family, shows God's amazing greatness. God orchestrated every event, using even the bad choices of Joseph's brothers to bring about His good plan. God is truly great, far above anything we can imagine. His greatness means He is in control of all things, and He works all things for His purposes.

 **ACTIVITY**

Think about something in nature that shows God's greatness, like a vast ocean or a starry night sky. Draw a picture of something grand and awe-inspiring.

PRAYER

Great God, You are worthy of all praise. Thank You for Your greatness and for showing Your power in the world. Amen.

Chapter 94: God's Holiness

"But just as he who called you is holy, so be holy in all you do; for it is written: 'Be holy, because I am holy.'" - 1 Peter 1:15-16

Even though Joseph was surrounded by a pagan culture in Egypt, he remained true to God. He refused to sin against God when Potiphar's wife tempted him. This shows Joseph's respect for God's holiness. God is pure and set apart from sin. He desires us to live holy lives, too, by making choices that honor Him and stay away from what is wrong.

 # ACTIVITY

Think about a choice you can make today that will show you want to live a life that honors God. Write it down. Draw a clean, shining light, representing holiness.

_____

_____

_____

_____

_____

_____

_____

_____

_____

_____

PRAYER

Holy God, thank You for being perfectly pure. Help me to live a life that honors You and to make choices that reflect Your holiness. Amen.

Chapter 95: God's Justice

"For the Lord loves the just and will not forsake his faithful ones. Wrongdoers will be completely destroyed; the offspring of the wicked will perish." - Psalm 37:28

Joseph suffered injustice when he was falsely accused and imprisoned. God is a God of justice. He sees every wrong, and He will make things right in His time. While Joseph was in prison, God brought about justice by revealing the truth through dreams and raising Joseph to power. God's justice means He is always fair, and He will ultimately correct all wrongs. We can trust Him to bring justice.

 **ACTIVITY**

Think about a time you saw something that was unfair. How did it make you feel? Draw a simple balance scale, representing justice and fairness.

PRAYER

Just God, thank You for being fair and for loving justice. Help me to trust that You will make all things right in Your perfect time. Amen.

Chapter 96: God's Mercy

"Blessed are the merciful, for they will be shown mercy." - Matthew 5:7

Joseph showed great mercy to his brothers, even though they had hurt him deeply. He did not punish them or seek revenge. Instead, he forgave them and provided for them. This reflects God's own mercy towards us. God does not give us the punishment we deserve for our sins. Instead, He offers us forgiveness and a chance to be close to Him. We are called to be merciful to others, just as God is merciful to us.

 **ACTIVITY**

Think about someone who might need your mercy today. It could be a friend who made a mistake or a sibling who upset you. What is one way you can show them mercy?

 **PRAYER**

Merciful God, thank You for Your amazing mercy towards me. Help me to be merciful and compassionate to others, just as You are. Amen.

Chapter 97: God's Grace

"For it is by grace you have been saved, through faith—and this is not from yourselves, it is the gift of God." - Ephesians 2:8

Grace is a gift we receive that we do not earn or deserve. Joseph received God's grace when he was given favor in Potiphar's house and in prison. We receive God's greatest grace through Jesus. We do not deserve His love or forgiveness, but God freely gives it to us because of His great love. God's grace is a powerful reminder of His kindness and generosity towards us.

 **ACTIVITY**

Think about a gift you received that you did not expect or earn. How did it make you feel? Draw a wrapped gift box, representing God's grace.

PRAYER

Gracious God, thank You for Your wonderful grace. Thank You for giving me gifts I do not deserve. Help me to live in Your grace and share it with others. Amen.

Chapter 98: God's Unchanging Character

"Jesus Christ is the same yesterday and today and forever." - Hebrews 13:8

Through all the many years and changing circumstances in Joseph's life, God remained the same. His character did not change. He was always powerful, wise, good, holy, and faithful. God is unchanging. He is the same yesterday, today, and forever. This truth gives us stability and security. We can always count on God to be who He says He is.

 **ACTIVITY**

Think about something in nature that stays the same, like the sun always rising in the east. How does that remind you of God's unchanging nature? Draw a steady, unchanging mountain.

PRAYER

Unchanging God, thank You for being constant and true. Help me to find my security in Your unchanging character. Amen.

Chapter 99: God's Sovereignty

"The Lord does whatever pleases him, in the heavens and on the earth, in the seas and all their depths." - Psalm 135:6

God's sovereignty means He is in control of everything. He is the supreme ruler over all creation and all events. Joseph's story clearly shows God's sovereignty. Even when Joseph's brothers made evil choices, God used those choices to bring about His greater plan of saving many lives. God is always working behind the scenes, orchestrating everything to fulfill His purposes. We can rest in His complete control.

 **ACTIVITY**

Think about a time when something unexpected happened, and it turned out to be part of a bigger, good plan. How did that feel? Draw a large hand gently guiding many small pieces, representing God's control.

PRAYER

Sovereign God, thank You for being in control of all things. Help me to trust Your plan and Your rule over my life and the world. Amen.

Chapter 100: Trusting God Completely

"Trust in the Lord with all your heart and lean not on your own understanding." - Proverbs 3:5

Joseph's life is a testament to trusting God completely. He trusted God when he was sold, when he was in prison, and when he was raised to power. He trusted God's plan, even when it was painful. Trusting God completely means giving Him all our worries, fears, and hopes, knowing He will take care of us. It means believing in His goodness and His power in every situation.

 **ACTIVITY**

Think about one area of your life where you need to trust God more. Write it down. Draw a picture of a tightrope walker, symbolizing complete trust and balance.

PRAYER

Trustworthy God, I want to trust You completely. Help me to give You all my worries and to lean on Your understanding in every part of my life. Amen.

Chapter 101: Moses Is Born

"But when she could no longer hide him, she got a papyrus basket for him and coated it with tar and pitch. Then she placed the baby in it and put it among the reeds along the bank of the Nile." - Exodus 2:3

Many years after Joseph died, Jacob's descendants multiplied until they became a vast group of people living inside Egypt. A new Pharaoh came to power who did not remember Joseph. He was afraid of how many Israelites there were, so he made them slaves and treated them cruelly. Pharaoh even ordered that every newborn Israelite boy be thrown into the Nile River to ensure they would not survive.

A brave mother, Jochebed, hid her baby boy, Moses, in a basket in the river. God protected Moses, and Pharaoh's own daughter found him and raised him. This shows God's amazing way of protecting His people, even in dangerous times.

 **ACTIVITY**

Imagine you are trying to keep a secret safe. How would you do it? Draw a simple basket floating on water, representing baby Moses' escape.

PRAYER

Protecting God, thank You for watching over us, even when we are in danger. Thank You for protecting Moses. Help me to trust Your care for me. Amen.

Chapter 102: The Burning Bush

"There the angel of the Lord appeared to him in flames of fire from within a bush. Moses saw that though the bush was on fire it did not burn up." - Exodus 3:2

Moses grew up in Pharaoh's palace, but he knew he was an Israelite. After some trouble, he ran away to the desert and became a shepherd. One day, while tending sheep, Moses saw a strange sight: a bush was burning, but it was not burning up! As Moses went to look closer, God spoke to him from the bush. God told Moses that He had heard the cries of His people in Egypt and was sending Moses to lead them out of slavery. This was a surprising call for Moses, but God chose him for a big task.

 **ACTIVITY**

Imagine you see something amazing and unusual. How would you react? Draw a simple bush with flames, but make it look like the bush is not being harmed.

PRAYER

Amazing God, thank You for speaking to us and for calling us to do important things. Help me to listen when You call and to be ready to obey. Amen.

Chapter 103: God Calls Moses

"God said to Moses, 'I AM WHO I AM. This is what you are to say to the Israelites: "I AM has sent me to you."'" - Exodus 3:14

Moses felt nervous about going back to Pharaoh and leading God's people. He made excuses, saying he was not a good speaker and asking who he should say sent him. God answered all of Moses' concerns. God told Moses His name: "I AM WHO I AM," meaning God is always present and always true to Himself. God promised to be with Moses and give him the words to say. God also gave Moses signs to show the Israelites that He had sent him. When God calls us, He also equips us.

 **ACTIVITY**

Think about a time you felt nervous about doing something new or difficult. What helped you feel brave? Write down one thing God promised Moses that would make him feel brave.

PRAYER

God, thank You for calling me and for promising to be with me. Help me to be brave and to trust that You will give me what I need to do Your will. Amen.

Chapter 104: Pharaoh's Hard Heart

"But Pharaoh said, 'Who is the Lord, that I should obey him and let Israel go? I do not know the Lord and I will not let Israel go.'" - *Exodus 5:2*

Moses and his brother Aaron went to Pharaoh and told him God's command: "Let my people go!" Pharaoh refused. He did not know God and did not want to lose his slaves. Pharaoh made the Israelites work even harder. God allowed Pharaoh's heart to become hard so that He could show His mighty power to all of Egypt and to His own people. Pharaoh's stubbornness set the stage for God to do amazing miracles.

 **ACTIVITY**

Think about a time someone was very stubborn and would not listen. How did that make you feel? Draw a simple, frowning face, representing Pharaoh's hard heart.

PRAYER

Powerful God, thank You for showing Your strength. Help me to have a soft heart that listens to You and obeys Your commands. Amen.

Chapter 105: The Ten Plagues

"Then the Lord said to Moses, 'Go to Pharaoh and say to him, "This is what the Lord, the God of the Hebrews, says: Let my people go, so that they may worship me."'" - Exodus 9:1

Because Pharaoh refused to let God's people go, God sent ten terrible plagues upon Egypt. These were not just random bad things. Each plague showed God's power over the gods of Egypt and over all of creation. There were plagues of blood, frogs, gnats, flies, diseased livestock, boils, hail, locusts, darkness, and finally, the death of the firstborn. Each plague was a clear message from God to Pharaoh and to the Egyptians. God was showing them who the true God is.

 # ACTIVITY

Imagine ten different kinds of difficult problems. Which one would be the hardest to deal with? Draw a simple picture for one of the plagues, like frogs or flies.

PRAYER

Mighty God, thank You for showing Your power. Help me to always know that You are the one true God and that You are in control of everything. Amen.

Chapter 106: The Passover

"The blood will be a sign for you on the houses where you are, and when I see the blood, I will pass over you. No destructive plague will touch you when I strike Egypt." - Exodus 12:13

The tenth and final plague was the most severe: the death of the firstborn in every Egyptian home. God gave the Israelites a way to be saved. Each family was to sacrifice a lamb, put its blood on the doorframes of their houses, and eat a special meal. When the angel of death passed through Egypt, he would "pass over" the houses marked with the blood. This event is called the Passover. It reminds us that sin brings death, but God provides a way of salvation through blood, pointing to Jesus, the Lamb of God.

 **ACTIVITY**

Think about a time you felt safe because of a special sign or protection. Draw a simple doorframe with a mark on it, representing the blood of the lamb.

PRAYER

Saving God, thank You for providing a way of salvation. Thank You for the Passover, which reminds me of Jesus, our Savior. Amen.

Chapter 107: Crossing the Red Sea

"Then Moses stretched out his hand over the sea, and all that night the Lord drove the sea back with a strong east wind and turned it into dry land. The waters were divided, and the Israelites went through the sea on dry ground, with a wall of water on their right and on their left." - Exodus 14:21-22

After the tenth plague, Pharaoh finally let the Israelites go. They quickly left Egypt, but Pharaoh soon changed his mind and chased after them with his army. The Israelites were trapped between Pharaoh's army and the Red Sea. They were very scared. Moses cried out to God, and God told Moses to stretch his staff over the sea. The waters parted, creating a dry path for the Israelites to walk through! When the Egyptians tried to follow, the waters crashed back, and Pharaoh's army was defeated. This was an incredible miracle that showed God's mighty power to save His people.

 # ACTIVITY

Imagine walking through the middle of a sea with walls of water on both sides! How would that feel? Draw a wavy line split in the middle, showing the Red Sea parting.

PRAYER

Powerful God, thank You for Your amazing power to save. Thank You for making a way where there seems to be no way. Help me to trust You in impossible situations. Amen.

Chapter 108: God's Deliverance

"Moses answered the people, "Do not be afraid. Stand firm and you will see the deliverance the Lord will bring you today. The Egyptians you see today you will never see again. 14 The Lord will fight for you; you need only to be still."" — *Exodus 14:13-14*

Pharaoh's chariots thundered closer, waves lashed the shore, and the Israelites seemed trapped between an army and a sea. In that impossible moment God stepped in: a pillar of cloud slid behind His people like a shield, the wind roared all night, and walls of water rose to open a dry path straight through the Red Sea.

Every Israelite, young and old, strong and weary, walked between towering waves and reached the far shore safely. When the Egyptians rushed in after them, the waters crashed back and the threat was gone.

This rescue shows two sides of God's power. First, He judges persistent evil, crushing the might of Pharaoh, who had enslaved and pursued His people. Second, He delivers those who trust Him, even when escape appears impossible. Whenever you feel hemmed in by fear, trouble, or unfair treatment, remember the sea that split in answer to God's command. He still fights for His people, opening roads no one else can see and turning obstacles into avenues of freedom.

 **ACTIVITY**

Think about a time you felt rescued from a difficult situation. How did it feel? Draw a simple drawing of someone being freed from chains, representing deliverance.

PRAYER

Delivering God, thank You for rescuing me from trouble. You are my strength and my shield. Help me to praise You for Your deliverance. Amen.

Chapter 109: Singing to God

"Then Moses and the Israelites sang this song to the Lord: 'I will sing to the Lord, for he is highly exalted. The horse and its rider he has hurled into the sea.'" - Exodus 15:1

After crossing the Red Sea and seeing Pharaoh's army defeated, the Israelites were filled with joy and relief. Moses and the people sang a song of praise to God, celebrating His victory and His mighty power. They sang about how God is great and how He had triumphed. When God does amazing things in our lives, it is good to respond with praise and thankfulness. Singing to God is a wonderful way to express our gratitude and joy.

 ACTIVITY

Think about your favorite song. How does music make you feel? Sing a short song of praise to God, or just hum a happy tune, thinking about His goodness.

 PRAYER

Praising God, thank You for Your mighty acts and for Your deliverance. Help me to always praise You with a joyful heart. Amen.

Chapter 110: Manna from Heaven

"Then the Lord said to Moses, 'I will rain down bread from heaven for you. The people are to go out each day and gather enough for that day.'" - Exodus 16:4

The Israelites were now free, but they were in a vast desert. Soon, they ran out of food and began to complain to Moses and Aaron. God heard their complaints and showed His loving care. Every morning, except on the Sabbath, God sent a special food from heaven called manna. It looked like small white flakes and tasted like wafers with honey. God provided this daily food for forty years in the desert. This shows God's faithfulness to provide for His people, even in the most challenging places.

 **ACTIVITY**

Imagine waking up every morning and finding food magically on the ground! How would that feel? Draw a simple picture of small flakes falling from the sky, representing manna.

PRAYER

Providing God, thank You for giving us our daily food. Thank You for providing for the Israelites in the desert. Help me to trust You to meet all my needs. Amen.

Chapter 111: Water from the Rock

"The Lord said to Moses, 'Go in front of the people and take with you some of the elders of Israel. Take in your hand the staff with which you struck the Nile, and go. I will stand there before you by the rock at Horeb. Strike the rock, and water will come out of it for the people to drink.' Moses did this in the sight of the elders of Israel." - Exodus 17:5-6

After leaving Egypt, the Israelites faced another problem in the desert: no water. They complained again, grumbling against Moses and God. God told Moses to strike a rock with his staff. When Moses obeyed, water gushed out of the rock, enough for everyone to drink! This was another incredible miracle that showed God's power to provide for His people's needs, even in a dry and barren land. God is always able to provide for us, no matter how impossible the situation seems.

 **ACTIVITY**

Imagine being very thirsty and suddenly seeing water appear from a rock. How amazing would that be? Draw a simple rock with water flowing out of it.

PRAYER

Providing God, thank You for giving us water and for meeting all our needs. Help me to trust You to provide, even when I feel thirsty or in need. Amen.

Chapter 112: God Provides

"And my God will meet all your needs according to the riches of his glory in Christ Jesus." - Philippians 4:19

The stories of manna and water from the rock show us a big truth: God provides for His people. He knows what we need before we even ask, and He is faithful to give it. Sometimes His provision is a miracle, and sometimes it is through ordinary ways, like our parents providing food and clothes. God's provision is a sign of His constant love and care for us. We can always count on Him to take care of us.

 **ACTIVITY**

Make a list of five things God has provided for you today. It could be food, a safe place to sleep, fresh air, or a friend. Thank God for each one.

 **PRAYER**

Loving God, thank You for always providing for my needs. Help me to be grateful for all Your blessings and to trust You for all that I need. Amen.

Chapter 113: The Ten Commandments: No Other Gods

"I am the Lord your God, who brought you out of Egypt, out of the land of slavery. You shall have no other gods before me." - Exodus 20:2-3

After the Israelites left Egypt, God brought them to Mount Sinai. There, God spoke directly to them and gave them special rules called the Ten Commandments. The first commandment is: "You shall have no other gods before me." This means God is the only true God, and we should worship only Him. We should not put anything else in God's place, like money, popularity, or even our favorite toys. God deserves our full love and attention.

 **ACTIVITY**

Think about something you really love. Is it more important to you than God? Draw a picture of a single, shining star, representing God as the only true God.

PRAYER

Dear God, thank You for being the one true God. Help me to love You above everything else and to worship only You. Amen.

Chapter 114: The Ten Commandments: No Idols

"You shall not make for yourself an image in the form of anything in heaven above or on the earth beneath or in the waters below. You shall not bow down to them or worship them; for I, the Lord your God, am a jealous God, punishing the children for the sin of the parents to the third and fourth generation of those who hate me," - Exodus 20:4-5

The second commandment is: "You shall not make for yourself an idol." An idol is anything we worship or give our devotion to instead of God. It could be a statue, a picture, or even an idea. God wants us to worship Him in spirit and truth, not through things we can see or touch. He wants our hearts to be fully devoted to Him alone.

 ## ACTIVITY

Think about something that people sometimes care about more than God. Draw a line through it, showing that God should be first.

PRAYER

God, thank You for wanting my whole heart. Help me to worship You alone and not to let anything else take Your place in my life. Amen.

Chapter 115: The Ten Commandments: God's Name

"You shall not misuse the name of the Lord your God, for the Lord will not hold anyone guiltless who misuses his name." - Exodus 20:7

The third commandment says: "You shall not misuse the name of the Lord your God." God's name is holy and special. We should use it with respect and honor, not in anger, jokes, or carelessly. Using God's name properly shows we respect Him and His greatness. When we speak His name, we should remember who He is.

 ACTIVITY

Think about someone you respect very much. How do you speak their name? Practice saying "God" or "Lord" with reverence. Write down one way you can use God's name with respect today.

PRAYER

Holy God, thank You for Your amazing name. Help me to always use Your name with respect and to honor You in all my words. Amen.

Chapter 116: The Ten Commandments: The Sabbath

"Remember the Sabbath day by keeping it holy. Six days you shall labor and do all your work, but the seventh day is a sabbath to the Lord your God. On it you shall not do any work, neither you, nor your son or daughter, nor your male or female servant, nor your animals, nor any foreigner residing in your towns." - Exodus 20:8-10

The fourth commandment tells us to "Remember the Sabbath day by keeping it holy." God worked for six days creating the world, and on the seventh day, He rested. He set this day apart as a special time for rest and worship. For us, this means taking time each week to rest from our work, spend time with God, and gather with other believers to worship Him. It is a gift from God to refresh our bodies and spirits.

 # ACTIVITY

What is your favorite way to rest and relax? Draw a picture of a peaceful scene, like someone reading the Bible or spending time with family, representing Sabbath rest.

PRAYER

Resting God, thank You for the gift of the Sabbath. Help me to set aside time each week to rest, worship You, and grow closer to You. Amen.

Chapter 117: The Ten Commandments: Honor Parents

"Honor your father and your mother, so that you may live long in the land the Lord your God is giving you." - Exodus 20:12

The fifth commandment says: "Honor your father and your mother." This means treating our parents with respect, listening to them, and obeying their instructions. Even when we disagree, we should show them honor. God gave us parents to care for us and guide us. When we honor them, we are also honoring God, who gave them to us. This commandment comes with a promise of long life.

 ACTIVITY

Think about one way you can show honor to your parents today. Maybe it is by doing a chore without being asked, or by listening carefully when they speak. Do that one thing.

 PRAYER

God, thank You for my parents. Help me to honor and respect them in all that I do and say. Amen.

Chapter 118: The Ten Commandments: Do Not Murder

"You shall not murder." - Exodus 20:13

The sixth commandment is: "You shall not murder." This commandment protects human life, which is precious to God. Every person is made in God's image, so taking a life is a serious sin against God. God wants us to love and respect each other.

ACTIVITY

Think about how precious life is. What is one way you can show love and respect for someone else's life today? Draw a picture of a heart, representing love for others.

PRAYER

God of Life, thank You for the gift of life. Help me to value every person and to show love and respect to everyone I meet. Amen.

Chapter 119: The Ten Commandments: Be Faithful

"You shall not commit adultery." - Exodus 20:14

The seventh commandment says: "You shall not commit adultery." This commandment protects the special relationship of marriage. God designed marriage to be a lifelong commitment between a husband and a wife. Being faithful in marriage means being loyal and true to your spouse. This commandment also reminds us to be pure in our thoughts and actions, respecting the special bonds God creates.

 # ACTIVITY

Think about what it means to be loyal to a friend or a team. How does loyalty make a relationship strong? Draw two rings linked together, symbolizing faithfulness in marriage.

PRAYER

Faithful God, thank You for designing marriage and for the importance of loyalty. Help me to be faithful in all my relationships and to live a pure life. Amen.

Chapter 120: The Ten Commandments: Do Not Steal

"You shall not steal." - Exodus 20:15

The eighth commandment is: "You shall not steal." Stealing means taking something that does not belong to you without permission. This commandment teaches us to respect other people's property and to be honest. God wants us to work hard for what we have and to be content with it. When we do not steal, we show respect for others and for God's laws.

 **ACTIVITY**

Think about something that belongs to you that you value. How would you feel if someone took it? Draw a simple image of a hand giving, representing honesty and generosity.

PRAYER

Honest God, thank You for teaching me to be honest. Help me to respect other people's property and to be content with what I have. Amen.

Chapter 121: The Ten Commandments: Do Not Lie

"You shall not give false testimony against your neighbor." - Exodus 20:16

The ninth commandment says: "You shall not give false testimony against your neighbor." This means we should not lie, especially when it harms someone else's reputation or causes them trouble. God is a God of truth, and He wants us to speak truthfully. Lying breaks trust and can cause much pain. When we tell the truth, we build strong relationships and honor God.

 **ACTIVITY**

Think about a time you told the truth even when it was difficult. How did that feel? Draw a speech bubble with a checkmark inside, representing truthfulness.

PRAYER

Truthful God, help me to always speak the truth. Guide my words so that they are honest and do not harm others. Amen.

Chapter 122: The Ten Commandments: Do Not Covet

"You shall not covet your neighbor's house. You shall not covet your neighbor's wife, or their male or female servant, their ox or donkey, or anything that belongs to your neighbor." - Exodus 20:17

The tenth and final commandment is: "You shall not covet." Coveting means wanting something eagerly. It is about what is in our hearts. God wants us to be content with what we have and to be happy for others when they have good things. This commandment reminds us that God sees our hearts and desires us to have a grateful spirit.

 **ACTIVITY**

Think about something you really want that someone else has. How can you be happy for them instead of wishing it was yours? Draw a happy face next to a picture of something you are thankful for that you already have.

PRAYER

Content God, thank You for all You have given me. Help me to be content and to be happy for others, not wanting what they have. Amen.

Chapter 123: Why God Gives Rules

"Keep my decrees and laws, for the person who obeys them will live by them. I am the Lord." - Leviticus 18:5

The Ten Commandments might seem like a lot of rules, but God gave them to us because He loves us. His rules are like a guide to help us live good lives, protect us from harm, and show us how to have a close relationship with Him and with each other. God's rules are not meant to make us unhappy. They are meant to bring us peace, joy, and a way to live that honors Him.

 # ACTIVITY

Think about a game you play that has rules. Why are those rules important for the game to be fun and fair? Draw a simple road sign with an arrow pointing the right way, representing God's rules as guidance.

PRAYER

Loving God, thank You for Your good rules that guide me. Help me to understand that Your laws are for my good and to obey them with a willing heart. Amen.

Chapter 124: The Tabernacle

"Then have them make a sanctuary for me, and I will dwell among them. Make this Tabernacle and all its furnishings exactly like the pattern I will show you." - Exodus 25:8-9

After giving the Ten Commandments, God gave Moses detailed instructions for building a special tent called the Tabernacle. This was a portable place of worship where God's presence would dwell among the Israelites as they traveled through the desert. Every part of the Tabernacle, from its design to the furniture inside, had a special meaning and pointed to God's holiness and His plan to be with His people.

 # ACTIVITY

Imagine building a very special place to meet with God. What would it look like? Draw a simple tent, representing the Tabernacle, with a cloud above it to show God's presence.

PRAYER

Present God, thank You for wanting to be with Your people. Help me to remember that You are always with me, and I can meet with You anywhere. Amen.

Chapter 125: God's Presence

"And I will dwell among the Israelites and be their God. They will know that I am the Lord their God, who brought them out of Egypt so that I might dwell among them. I am the Lord their God." - Exodus 29:45-46

The Tabernacle was a powerful reminder that God was present with His people. A cloud by day and a pillar of fire by night guided them and showed God's presence. Even though we do not have a physical Tabernacle today, God's presence is still with us through the Holy Spirit. We can experience His presence in our hearts when we trust in Jesus. Knowing God is always with us brings comfort and courage.

 **ACTIVITY**

Think about a time you felt someone's presence made you feel safe or happy. How did that feel? Draw a small, simple cloud or a flame, representing God's presence.

PRAYER

Present God, thank You for always being with me. Help me to feel Your presence and to find comfort and strength in knowing You are always near. Amen.

Chapter 126: The Priests

"Have Aaron your brother brought to you from among the Israelites, along with his sons Nadab and Abihu, Eleazar and Ithamar, so that they may serve me as priests." - Exodus 28:1

God chose Aaron, Moses' brother, and his sons to be priests. The priests had a very important job in the Tabernacle. They were to serve God, offer sacrifices for the people's sins, and teach God's laws. They helped the people connect with God. This system showed the Israelites that they needed someone to stand between them and a holy God because of their sin. This pointed forward to Jesus, our ultimate High Priest.

 **ACTIVITY**

Think about someone who helps you understand important rules or helps you connect with something important. Draw a simple figure with outstretched hands, representing a priest serving God and people.

PRAYER

God, thank You for those who serve You and teach Your Word. Thank You for Jesus, our perfect High Priest, who connects us to You. Amen.

Chapter 127: Sacrifices for Sin

"For the life of a creature is in the blood, and I have given it to you to make atonement for yourselves on the altar; it is the blood that makes atonement for one's life." - Leviticus 17:11

In the Tabernacle, people brought animals to be sacrificed to God. These sacrifices were a way for the Israelites to show sorrow for their sins and to ask for God's forgiveness. The blood of the animal covered their sins for a time. This system taught them that sin is serious and requires a penalty. All these sacrifices pointed to the ultimate sacrifice that Jesus would make one day, shedding His own blood to forgive our sins once and for all.

 **ACTIVITY**

Think about a time you said "I'm sorry" and truly meant it. How did that feel? Draw a simple cross, representing Jesus' ultimate sacrifice for our sins.

PRAYER

Forgiving God, thank You for providing a way for my sins to be forgiven. Thank You for Jesus, who made the perfect sacrifice for me. Amen.

Chapter 128: God's Holiness

"You are to distinguish between the holy and the common, and between the unclean and the clean." - Leviticus 10:10

The detailed instructions for the Tabernacle and the role of the priests and sacrifices all emphasized God's holiness. God is completely pure and set apart from sin. He cannot be around sin. This is why the Israelites had to follow so many rules to approach Him. God's holiness is a reminder of His perfect character and why sin is so serious. It also shows His incredible love that He provided a way for sinful people to come close to Him.

 **ACTIVITY**

Think about something that is perfectly clean and pure. How does that help you understand God's holiness? Draw a shining light, representing God's pure holiness.

PRAYER

Holy God, You are perfectly pure and set apart. Help me to understand Your holiness and to live in a way that honors You. Amen.

Chapter 129: The Spies Explore the Land

"The Lord said to Moses, 'Send some men to explore the land of Canaan, which I am giving to the Israelites. From each ancestral tribe send one of its leaders.'" - Numbers 13:1-2

After about a year at Mount Sinai, God told Moses to send twelve leaders, one from each tribe, to explore the land of Canaan, the land God had promised them. They were to see what the land was like, if the people were strong or weak, and if the towns were unwalled or fortified. They spent forty days exploring the land. This was an important step in preparing to enter the Promised Land.

 **ACTIVITY**

Imagine you are going on a scouting mission to a new place. What would you look for? Draw a simple map with a path leading to an unknown area.

PRAYER

Guiding God, thank You for leading Your people. Help me to be brave and ready to explore new things You have for me. Amen.

Chapter 130: Caleb and Joshua's Faith

"Then Caleb silenced the people before Moses and said, 'We should go up and take possession of the land, for we can certainly do it.'" - Numbers 13:30

The twelve spies returned from Canaan with their report. Ten of the spies brought a bad report. They said the land was good, but the people living there were giants, and their cities were strong. They were afraid and did not believe God could help them conquer the land.

Only two spies, Caleb and Joshua, brought a good report. They said, "We should go up and take possession of the land, for we can certainly do it." They trusted God's promise. This shows the difference between fear and faith.

 **ACTIVITY**

Think about a time you felt afraid to do something, but someone encouraged you to be brave. How did that help? Draw two thumbs up, representing Caleb and Joshua's positive report.

PRAYER

Thank You for Caleb and Joshua's example of faith. Help me to be brave and to trust Your promises, even when things look difficult. Amen.

Chapter 131: Consequences of Disobedience

"Not one of you will enter the land I swore with uplifted hand to make your home, except Caleb son of Jephunneh and Joshua son of Nun." - Numbers 14:30

Because the Israelites listened to the ten fearful spies and refused to trust God, they disobeyed God's command to enter the Promised Land. God declared that the entire generation who had doubted Him, except for Caleb and Joshua, would wander in the desert for forty years. They would not enter the land. This was a sad consequence of their disobedience and lack of faith. It shows that our choices have consequences, and disobeying God can lead to difficult paths.

 **ACTIVITY**

Think about a time you faced a consequence for a choice you made. What did you learn? Draw a winding path that seems to go on and on, representing the Israelites' wandering.

PRAYER

God, help me to trust You and obey You, so I can avoid difficult consequences. Teach me to learn from the mistakes of others. Amen.

Chapter 132: God's Patience with His People

"The Lord is compassionate and gracious, slow to anger, abounding in love." - Psalm 103:8

Even though the Israelites rebelled and were punished with forty years in the desert, God did not abandon them. He continued to provide manna and water. He continued to lead them with the cloud and fire. God showed incredible patience with His complaining and disobedient people. His patience is a wonderful quality. He gives us many chances to learn and to turn back to Him.

 **ACTIVITY**

Think about a time you had to be very patient with someone. How did that feel? Draw a picture of a patient teacher helping a student.

PRAYER

Patient God, thank You for Your amazing patience with me. Help me to learn from my mistakes and to always turn back to You. Amen.

Chapter 133: The Bronze Snake

"The Lord said to Moses, 'Make a snake and put it up on a pole; anyone who is bitten who looks at it will live.'" - Numbers 21:8

During their time in the desert, the Israelites complained about God and Moses again. God sent poisonous snakes among them, and many people were bitten and died. When the people cried out for help, God told Moses to make a bronze snake and put it on a pole. Anyone who looked at the bronze snake would live.

This was a simple act of faith. It was God's way of healing them, and it pointed forward to Jesus, who would be lifted up on a cross so that everyone who looks to Him in faith can have eternal life.

 **ACTIVITY**

Imagine you are very sick, and the only way to get better is to look at something. Would you trust it? Draw a simple snake on a pole.

PRAYER

Healing God, thank You for providing a way for us to be healed. Thank You for Jesus, who was lifted up for us. Help me to look to Him in faith. Amen.

Chapter 134: Moses' Last Instructions

"These are the commands, decrees and laws the Lord your God directed me to teach you to observe in the land that you are entering to possess." - *Deuteronomy 6:1*

As the forty years in the desert came to an end, Moses, who had faithfully led the Israelites for so long, knew he would not enter the Promised Land. Before he died, Moses gathered the people and reminded them of all God had done for them. He repeated God's laws and urged them to obey God with all their heart. He wanted them to remember God's faithfulness and to teach their children to love and obey God. This shows Moses' deep care for God's people.

ACTIVITY

Think about the most important advice someone has ever given you. What was it? Draw a picture of a wise person teaching a group of listeners.

PRAYER

God, thank You for giving us Your laws and for wise leaders like Moses. Help me to remember Your commands and to teach them to others. Amen.

Chapter 135: God's Promises Fulfilled

"Not one of all the Lord's good promises to Israel failed; every one was fulfilled." - Joshua 21:45

Throughout the journey of the Israelites, from Abraham to Moses, God made many promises. He promised a land, a great nation, and a Savior. Even though the Israelites often struggled to obey, God remained faithful to His word. He brought them out of Egypt, provided for them in the desert, and prepared them to enter the Promised Land. This shows God's incredible faithfulness to fulfill every promise He makes, no matter how long it takes.

 # ACTIVITY

Think about a time a promise was fulfilled for you. How did that feel? Draw a simple checkmark next to a word "Promise," showing it is completed.

PRAYER

Faithful God, thank You for fulfilling all Your promises. Help me to trust that every word You speak is true and will come to pass. Amen.

Chapter 136: God's Covenant

"Now if you obey me fully and keep my covenant, then out of all nations you will be my treasured possession." - Exodus 19:5a

God made a special agreement, called a covenant, with the Israelites at Mount Sinai. He promised to be their God, and they promised to obey His laws. This covenant was a special relationship. God's covenants show His commitment to His people. Even when people break their side of the agreement, God remains faithful to His promises. This reminds us of God's enduring commitment to us.

 **ACTIVITY**

Think about a special agreement or promise you have with a friend or family member. How does that agreement make your relationship special? Draw two hands clasped together, symbolizing a covenant or agreement.

PRAYER

Covenant-Keeping God, thank You for Your faithful agreements with Your people. Help me to live in a way that honors my relationship with You. Amen.

Chapter 137: Remembering God's Goodness

"Remember how the Lord your God led you all the way in the wilderness these forty years, to humble and test you in order to know what was in your heart, whether or not you would keep his commands." - Deuteronomy 8:2

Moses urges the people to *remember on purpose*. In the wilderness, God led them step by step, teaching humility and trust. He fed them with manna, brought water from hard rock and guided them by a cloud and fire. None of that was an accident; it was God shaping their hearts to rely on Him rather than themselves.

When we look back at our own "desert" days, times we felt stuck, hungry for answers, or unsure where to go, we can spot quiet rescues and daily bread we might have missed. Remembering turns worry into worship and prepares us to obey today. God's past faithfulness isn't just a story; it's fuel for present trust and future courage.

ACTIVITY

Think about three good things God has done for you in your life. Write them down. Draw a simple picture of a memory, like a happy face or a heart.

PRAYER

Grateful God, thank You for all Your goodness in my life. Help me to always remember Your faithfulness and to be thankful for Your blessings. Amen.

Chapter 138: Following God's Commands

"If you fully obey the Lord your God and carefully follow all his commands I give you today, the Lord your God will set you high above all the nations on earth." - Deuteronomy 28:1

God repeatedly called Israel to *obey* not as busywork, but as a way of life that matched His heart. His commands taught them how to worship Him, treat neighbors fairly, guard the poor, rest each week, and celebrate gratitude, practices meant for their good.

Obedience is how love looks in action: we trust His wisdom more than our own and choose His ways in daily decisions (how we speak, share, tell the truth, and show kindness). When we walk this path, we don't earn God's love, we enjoy the blessings built into His design: a clear conscience, stronger communities, and a life that points others to Him.

 # ACTIVITY

Think about one of God's commands you learned today (like "Do not lie" or "Honor your parents"). What is one way you can follow that command in your life today?

PRAYER

Obedient God, help me to follow Your commands with a willing heart. Guide me to live in a way that pleases You and brings You glory. Amen.

Chapter 139: God's Discipline

"For the Lord disciplines those he loves, as a father the son he delights in." - Proverbs 3:12

Sometimes, when the Israelites disobeyed, God disciplined them. Discipline is not punishment out of anger, but correction out of love. Just like a loving parent corrects a child, God disciplines us to teach us, to help us grow, and to bring us back to the right path. God's discipline shows His care for us and His desire for us to live in a way that is good for us.

 **ACTIVITY**

Think about a time you were corrected, and it helped you learn something important. How did that feel later? Draw a simple picture of a hand guiding another hand, representing loving discipline.

PRAYER

Loving God, thank You for disciplining me when I need it. Help me to learn from Your correction and to grow closer to You. Amen.

Chapter 140: God's Enduring Love

"The Lord appeared to us in the past, saying: 'I have loved you with an everlasting love; I have drawn you with unfailing kindness.'" - Jeremiah 31:3

Despite the Israelites' repeated disobedience and grumbling in the desert, God's love for them never ended. His love is enduring. It lasts forever. This is a powerful truth for us, too. Even when we make mistakes, God's love for us remains. We can always return to Him, knowing His love is constant and waiting for us.

Think of a compass. No matter how many wrong turns you take, the needle always points north. God's love is like that, constant, reliable, and pointing you back to Him. When you realize you've wandered, stop, talk to God, say you're sorry, and ask for His help. He's not waiting to push you away; He's waiting to welcome you and walk with you.

 ACTIVITY

Think about something that lasts a very long time, like a strong tree or a big river. How does that remind you of God's enduring love? Draw a large, unchanging heart.

PRAYER

Enduring God, thank You for Your everlasting love that never fails. Help me to rest in Your constant love and to love You back. Amen.

Chapter 141: Learning from History

"These things happened to them as examples and were written down as warnings for us, on whom the culmination of the ages has come." - 1 Corinthians 10:11

The stories of the Israelites in the desert are not just old tales. They are lessons for us today. We can learn from their mistakes and from God's faithfulness to them. History helps us understand God's character and how He interacts with people. By studying these stories, we can avoid similar pitfalls and grow stronger in our own faith journey.

One simple way to use these lessons is to practice remembering: make a "God's Help" list of times He provided (big or small), tell those stories at meals, and thank Him out loud. Then practice responding: choose one small act of trust each day, obey quickly, tell the truth, show gratitude instead of grumbling, or share what you have. As we remember and respond, our faith gets steadier, and we walk forward with the God who still leads step by step.

ACTIVITY

Think about a historical event you learned about in school. What lesson did you take from it? Draw a simple timeline with a few key moments marked on it.

PRAYER

Wise God, thank You for the lessons in Your Word. Help me to learn from the stories of the past and to apply Your truths to my life today. Amen.

Chapter 142: God's Ways Are Best

*"For my thoughts are not your thoughts, neither are your ways my ways,'
declares the Lord." - Isaiah 55:8*

The Israelites often tried to do things their own way, which led to
trouble. God's ways are always best, even when they seem difficult or
different from what we want. His ways lead to peace, joy, and true life.
When we choose God's path, we are choosing wisdom and blessing.
Trusting God's ways means surrendering our own desires to His perfect
will.

One simple way to practice this is to pause and ask, "What would
please God here?" before you act or speak. Choose gratitude instead of
grumbling, honesty instead of shortcuts, kindness instead of getting even,
and prayer instead of panic. These small, everyday choices train our
hearts to walk in God's ways, and over time, they build the kind of
steady, joyful life that His wisdom promises.

 **ACTIVITY**

Think about a time you chose your own way, and it did not work out well. Then think about a time you followed good advice, and it worked out great. Draw a happy face on a path labeled "God's Way."

PRAYER

God, Your ways are perfect. Help me to choose Your path and to trust that Your plans for me are always the best. Amen.

Chapter 143: God's Law Is Good

"The law of the Lord is perfect, refreshing the soul. The statutes of the Lord are trustworthy, making wise the simple." - Psalm 19:7

The Ten Commandments and all of God's laws are good. They show us God's perfect character and what a right relationship with Him and others looks like. The law is like a mirror that shows us our sin, but it is also a guide for how to live. God's law is not a burden; it is a gift that leads to life and blessing when followed.

Like road signs, God's commands keep us from danger and point us toward what is loving and fair for others. When we find obedience hard, they remind us to ask God for help and choose what is right even when it's tough.

ACTIVITY

Think about a rule that helps keep a game fair and fun. How is God's law like that? Draw a simple open book with a heart on the page, representing God's good law.

PRAYER

Good God, thank You for Your perfect law. Help me to understand and love Your commands, knowing they are good for me. Amen.

Chapter 144: The Importance of Obedience

"If you love me, keep my commands." - John 14:15

Throughout the Old Testament, God emphasized the importance of obedience. When the Israelites obeyed, they were blessed. When they disobeyed, they faced consequences. Obedience is not just following rules blindly. It is an act of love and trust towards God. When we obey God, we show that we trust His wisdom and love. Obedience brings us closer to God.

 ## ACTIVITY

Think about a time you obeyed someone, and it led to a good outcome. How did that feel? Draw a simple path with footsteps, showing the journey of obedience.

PRAYER

Obedient God, help me to obey Your commands with a joyful heart. I want to show my love for You through my obedience. Amen.

Chapter 145: God's Steadfastness

"The steadfast love of the Lord never ceases; his mercies never come to an end; they are new every morning; great is your faithfulness." - Lamentations 3:22-23

God's steadfastness means He is firm, unwavering, and loyal. He does not change His mind or His character. Even when the Israelites were unfaithful, God remained steadfast in His promises and His love for them. We can always count on God to be the same, yesterday, today, and forever. His steadfastness is a rock we can stand on.

When everything around you changes, friends, feelings, plans, He stays steady like bedrock under your feet. Lean on that steadiness by praying, keeping your promises, and choosing what's right even when it's hard.

 **ACTIVITY**

Think about something that is very solid and does not move, like a large tree or a big rock. How does that remind you of God's steadfastness? Draw a strong, unmoving rock.

PRAYER

Steadfast God, thank You for Your unchanging love and faithfulness. Help me to find my security in Your steadfast character. Amen.

Chapter 146: God's Plans Are Greater

"For my thoughts are not your thoughts, neither are your ways my ways,'
declares the Lord. 'As the heavens are higher than the earth, so are my
ways higher than your ways and my thoughts than your thoughts.'" - Isaiah
55:8-9

The Israelites often had their own ideas about how things should go,
but God's plans were always greater. His plans included bringing them
out of slavery, providing for them, and leading them to a promised land.
God's plans for us are also far greater than anything we can imagine. We
can trust that He is working out something amazing, even when we
cannot see the whole picture.

When you're unsure of what comes next, pause and ask God to lead
you step by step. Choose small acts of trust, such as obey quickly, give

thanks instead of grumbling, and do the next right thing. Over time, these little choices become a pathway where you can see His bigger, better plan unfolding.

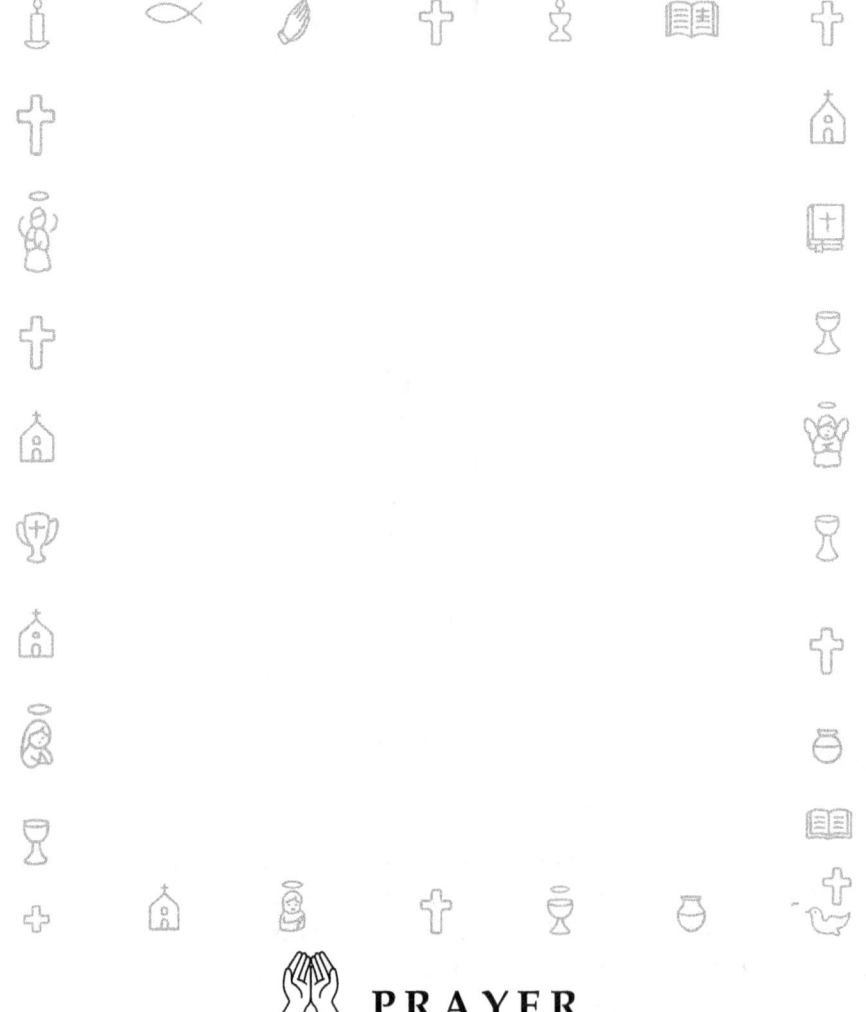 **ACTIVITY**

Imagine you are planning a small party. Now imagine someone else is planning a huge, amazing festival. How is God's plan like the bigger festival? Draw a small thought bubble and a much larger one next to it.

PRAYER

God, Your plans are so much greater than mine. Help me to trust Your big picture and to surrender my plans to Your perfect will. Amen.

Chapter 147: God's Perfect Timing

"He has made everything beautiful in its time. He has also set eternity in the human heart; yet no one can fathom what God has done from beginning to end." - Ecclesiastes 3:11

We saw in Joseph's story that God's timing is perfect. The Israelites also experienced God's perfect timing in their deliverance from Egypt and their journey through the desert. God knows exactly when to act, when to provide, and when to move us forward. We can rest in the knowledge that God's timing is always right, even when we feel impatient.

When waiting feels hard, try this: tell God what you're hoping for, thank Him for what He's already done, and do the next right thing today. Like following a guide on a trail, take one step at a time, trusting that when it's time for the next turn, God will make the way clear.

 **ACTIVITY**

Think about a time when something happened at just the right moment. How did it feel? Draw a clock with a happy, smiling face, representing God's perfect timing.

PRAYER

God of perfect timing, thank You for knowing the best moment for everything. Help me to be patient and to trust Your timing in all areas of my life. Amen.

Chapter 148: God's Unfailing Love

"Give thanks to the Lord, for he is good; his love endures forever." -
Psalm 107:1

God's love for the Israelites, despite their grumbling and disobedience, was unfailing. Unfailing love means it never runs out, never gives up, and never stops. It is a constant, steady love. This is the kind of love God has for us. No matter what we do, His love for us remains strong and true. We can always return to His unfailing love.

Think of it like the sun that rises every morning: whether it's cloudy or clear, the sun is still there. In the same way, God's love keeps shining over us, even on our "cloudy" days. When we realize we've messed up, we can turn back to Him, say we're sorry, and start fresh, knowing His love hasn't moved an inch.

 **ACTIVITY**

Think about something that always works, no matter what, like the sun always rising. How does that remind you of God's unfailing love? Draw a heart with an arrow going through it, showing it keeps going.

PRAYER

Unfailing God, thank You for Your love that never ends. Help me to rest in Your constant love and to share that love with others. Amen.

Chapter 149: God's Compassion

"The Lord is gracious and compassionate, slow to anger and rich in love."
- Psalm 145:8

God showed great compassion for the Israelites in the desert. Even when they complained, He provided food and water. Compassion means feeling deeply for someone's suffering and wanting to help them. God is full of compassion for us. He understands our struggles, our weaknesses, and our needs. His compassion moves Him to act on our behalf.

We can practice that same compassion in our everyday lives. When someone is frustrated or afraid, we can listen, speak kindly, and find a simple way to help, just like God did for His people. And when we're the ones struggling, we can ask Him for help, trusting that He still sees, still cares, and will give us what we need at the right time.

 **ACTIVITY**

Think about a time you felt compassion for someone who was hurting. What did you do to help them? Draw a picture of a hand gently touching a sad face, representing compassion.

PRAYER

Compassionate God, thank You for understanding my needs and for caring for me. Help me to show compassion to others, just as You show it to me. Amen.

Chapter 150: God's Righteousness

"The Lord is righteous in all his ways and faithful in all he does." - Psalm 145:17

God is righteous, meaning He is always fair, just, and morally perfect. He always does what is right. His laws are righteous, and His judgments are righteous. The Ten Commandments are a reflection of God's righteous character. We can trust that God will always act in perfect fairness and goodness. His righteousness means we can rely on Him to always do what is right.

Think of God's righteousness like a perfectly straight line that builders use to keep a wall from leaning. His ways show us what's true and steady, and they help us set things right when we've done wrong: by telling the truth, making amends, and choosing fairness. When we follow His ways, our lives stand strong and our communities become safer and kinder places.

 **ACTIVITY**

Think about someone you know who is always fair and does the right thing. How does that make you trust them? Draw a simple scale that is perfectly balanced, representing righteousness and fairness.

PRAYER

Righteous God, thank You for always being fair and doing what is right. Help me to live a life that reflects Your righteousness and honors You. Amen.

Chapter 151: God's Justice

"For the Lord loves the just and will not forsake his faithful ones. Wrongdoers will be completely destroyed; the offspring of the wicked will perish." - Psalm 37:28

We learned that God is righteous, and He is also just. Justice means that God always acts in fairness and makes things right. When the Israelites disobeyed, there were consequences, showing God's justice. God's justice also means He will punish evil and reward good. We can trust that God sees all injustice and will bring about perfect justice in His time.

Knowing this shapes how we live. We tell the truth, treat people fairly, keep our promises, and speak up when others are being hurt. When we do wrong, we make it right and ask for forgiveness. And when unfair things happen, we bring them to God, trusting Him to act wisely and on time.

 **ACTIVITY**

Think about a time you saw something unfair happen. How did you wish it could be made right? Draw a simple gavel, symbolizing justice.

PRAYER

Just God, thank You for loving justice and for always doing what is right. Help me to trust that You will make all things fair in Your perfect time. Amen.

Chapter 152: God's Faithfulness in Trials

"God is faithful; he will not let you be tempted beyond what you can bear. But when you are tempted, he will also provide a way out so that you can endure it." - 1 Corinthians 10:13

The Israelites faced many trials in the desert: hunger, thirst, and fear. Through all these challenges, God remained faithful. He provided manna, water from the rock, and protected them from enemies. God's faithfulness in trials means He is with us through every difficult situation. He does not abandon us when things get tough. We can rely on His presence and His help during our own trials.

When you face something hard, try remembering your "manna moments", times God has helped you before. Tell Him what you need, thank Him for past help, and do the next right thing today. Like a guide in the wilderness, He will lead you step by step until the path is clear again.

 **ACTIVITY**

Think about a small trial you faced recently, like a difficult homework assignment or a disagreement with a friend. How did you get through it? Draw a strong hand holding a smaller hand, representing God's help in trials.

PRAYER

Faithful God, thank You for being with me in every trial. Help me to remember Your faithfulness and to trust You to provide a way through difficulties. Amen.

Chapter 153: God's Strength in Weakness

"But he said to me, "My grace is sufficient for you, for my power is made perfect in weakness." Therefore I will boast all the more gladly about my weaknesses, so that Christ's power may rest on me.'" - 2 Corinthians 12:9

Moses often felt weak or inadequate for the big task God gave him. He felt he was not a good speaker, but God assured him of His strength. God's strength is made perfect in our weakness. When we feel weak, that is when God's power can shine through the most. We do not have to be strong enough on our own. We can rely on God's strength to accomplish His will through us.

When you feel nervous or not "good enough," try this: pause, take a deep breath, and pray, "God, be my strength." Then do the next small obedient step: say the kind word, try the hard homework, or speak up with honesty. Like Moses with his staff, God can use even simple, ordinary things in your hands to do something bigger than you imagined.

 **ACTIVITY**

Think about a time you felt you were not strong enough to do something. What happened? Draw a small figure leaning on a very large, strong pillar, representing leaning on God's strength.

PRAYER

Strong God, thank You for being strong when I am weak. Help me to lean on Your power and to trust You to work through me. Amen.

Chapter 154: God's Comfort in Sadness

"Praise be to the God and Father of our Lord Jesus Christ, the Father of compassion and the God of all comfort, who comforts us in all our troubles, so that we can comfort those in any trouble with the comfort we ourselves receive from God." - 2 Corinthians 1:3-4

The Israelites experienced sadness in the desert, grieving those who died and longing for the Promised Land. God provided comfort for them. God is the God of all comfort. When we are sad, hurting, or disappointed, we can turn to Him. He understands our feelings and offers peace and hope. His comfort helps us through difficult emotions.

One simple way to receive His comfort is to tell Him exactly how you feel, out loud or in a journal, and ask for His help. You can also lean on the good gifts He provides: a caring family member, a trusted friend, a quiet walk, or a favorite song that lifts your heart. As you keep coming to Him, He meets you with strength for today and gentle hope for tomorrow.

ACTIVITY

Think about a time you felt sad. What helped to comfort you? Draw a gentle hand wiping away a tear, representing God's comfort.

PRAYER

Comforting God, thank You for being with me when I am sad. Please comfort my heart and fill me with Your peace. Amen.

Chapter 155: God's Guidance in Confusion

"I will instruct you and teach you in the way you should go; I will counsel you with my loving eye on you." Psalm 32:8

The Israelites often did not know which way to go in the vast desert. God guided them with a cloud by day and a pillar of fire by night. He showed them exactly where to go. When we feel confused or unsure about what to do, God offers His guidance. We can pray, read His Word, and seek wise counsel. God promises to show us the right path.

Today, His guidance may not look like a glowing cloud, but He still leads through the wisdom of the Bible, a quiet nudge in our hearts, and the wise advice of trusted adults. When you're unsure, pause and pray, "God, show me the next right step," then listen and take that step. Over time, those small steps add up to a clear path.

 **ACTIVITY**

Imagine you are lost in a maze. How would it feel to have someone tell you the way out? Draw a simple arrow pointing the way on a winding path.

PRAYER

Guiding God, thank You for showing me the way when I am confused. Help me to listen for Your voice and to follow Your direction in my life. Amen.

Chapter 156: God's Peace in Storms

"You will keep in perfect peace those whose minds are steadfast, because they trust in you." - Isaiah 26:3

Life in the desert could be like a storm, with challenges and dangers. God provided peace for the Israelites, even in those stormy times. God offers us peace that is not dependent on our circumstances. It is a peace that comes from knowing He is in control. When we face our own "storms" in life, we can find calm in God's presence and His promises.

When worries start to swirl, pause to breathe and talk to God about what's scaring you. Thank Him for one good thing today, remember how He's helped you before, and ask Him to guide your next small step. His peace doesn't always remove the storm right away, but it steadies your heart until the skies clear.

 **ACTIVITY**

Think about a time you felt calm even when things around you were chaotic. What helped you feel that way? Draw a calm face in the middle of swirling lines, representing peace in a storm.

PRAYER

God of Peace, thank You for the peace You offer, even in difficult times. Help me to trust You and to find Your calm in my heart. Amen.

Chapter 157: God's Joy in Hardship

"The Lord is my strength and my shield; in him my heart trusts, and I am helped. My heart leaps for joy, and with my song I praise him." - Psalm 28:7

Even though the Israelites faced hardships in the desert, there were moments of great joy, like crossing the Red Sea or receiving the Ten Commandments. God brings joy even in difficult circumstances. Joy is a gift from God that gives us strength. We can find joy in God's presence, His goodness, and His faithfulness, even when life is hard.

Joy grows when we practice it: celebrate small wins, sing a thankful song, or share a story of how God helped you today. The more we notice and name His kindness, the more our hearts learn to rejoice, even in the middle of tough days.

 **ACTIVITY**

Think about a time you found joy in a surprising place or during a difficult time. What brought you that joy? Draw a happy face with a small sun shining on it.

PRAYER

Joyful God, thank You for bringing joy even in hardship. Help me to find my joy in You and to praise You in all circumstances. Amen.

Chapter 158: God's Hope for Tomorrow

"For I know the plans I have for you,' declares the Lord, 'plans to prosper you and not to harm you, plans to give you hope and a future.'" - Jeremiah 29:11

Despite their long journey in the desert, the Israelites had hope for tomorrow because God had promised them a land flowing with milk and honey. God always gives us hope for the future. He promises us a future with Him, free from pain and sorrow. This hope helps us keep going, even when today is difficult. We can look forward to what God has planned.

When hope feels small, practice noticing God's help today, write down one thing He provided, thank Him for it, and share it with someone. Then take the next right step, trusting that the same God who guided the Israelites is guiding you toward His good future, one day at a time.

 **ACTIVITY**

Think about something you are looking forward to in the future. How does that hope make you feel? Draw a simple path leading towards a bright horizon.

PRAYER

God of Hope, thank You for giving me hope for tomorrow and for a future with You. Help me to hold onto Your promises and to live with hope each day. Amen.

Chapter 159: God's Presence Always

"Keep your lives free from the love of money and be content with what you have, because God has said, "Never will I leave you; never will I forsake you." - Hebrews 13:5

The cloud and pillar of fire were visible signs of God's presence with the Israelites in the desert. They knew God was always with them. Today, God's presence is with us through the Holy Spirit. We do not need a cloud or fire to know He is near. He is always with us, guiding, comforting, and strengthening us. We are never truly alone.

When you need a reminder of this, pause and whisper, "God, I know You're here, help me listen." Pay attention to the gentle ways He leads: a verse that stands out, a calm feeling when you pray, a wise nudge to do what's right, or help that arrives at just the right time. Even when you don't *feel* anything, you can trust that He hasn't moved: His presence is steady and sure.

 ## ACTIVITY

Close your eyes and imagine God's loving presence surrounding you. Think about how comforting it is that He is always there. Draw a simple outline of a person with a glowing aura around them, representing God's presence.

PRAYER

Present God, thank You for always being with me. Help me to feel Your presence and to remember that You are always by my side. Amen.

Chapter 160: God's Amazing Grace

"For it is by grace you have been saved, through faith—and this is not from yourselves, it is the gift of God." - Ephesians 2:8

The Israelites often failed to obey God, yet God continued to show them grace. Grace is God's undeserved favor and kindness. They did not earn the manna, the water, or the deliverance. God gave it to them out of His grace. God's grace is amazing because it is freely given, even when we do not deserve it. It is through His grace that we can have a relationship with Him.

 **ACTIVITY**

Think about a time someone gave you a gift you did not earn. How did that make you feel? Draw a wrapped gift box with a ribbon, symbolizing God's amazing grace.

PRAYER

Gracious God, thank You for Your amazing grace. Thank You for giving me gifts I do not deserve. Help me to live in Your grace and to share it with others. Amen.

Chapter 161: Joshua Leads God's People

"Have I not commanded you? Be strong and courageous. Do not be afraid; do not be discouraged, for the Lord your God will be with you wherever you go." - Joshua 1:9

After Moses died, God chose Joshua to lead the Israelites into the Promised Land. This was a huge task, as the land was filled with strong nations. God told Joshua to be strong and courageous, promising to be with him wherever he went, just as He had been with Moses. Joshua trusted God and stepped into his new leadership role.

This shows that God equips those He calls and gives them courage.

 # ACTIVITY

Think about a time you had to be a leader or take on a new responsibility. How did it feel? Draw a simple figure leading a group of people, representing Joshua.

PRAYER

Courageous God, thank You for calling leaders and for being with them. Help me to be strong and brave in the tasks You give me, knowing You are with me. Amen.

Chapter 162: Crossing the Jordan River

"Now the Jordan is at flood stage all during harvest. Yet as soon as the priests who carried the ark reached the Jordan and their feet touched the water's edge, 16 the water from upstream stopped flowing. It piled up in a heap a great distance away, at a town called Adam in the vicinity of Zarethan, while the water flowing down to the Sea of the Arabah (that is, the Dead Sea) was completely cut off. So the people crossed over opposite Jericho." - Joshua 3:15-16

The Israelites needed to cross the Jordan River to enter the Promised Land, but it was at flood stage. God told Joshua to have the priests carry the Ark of the Covenant into the river. As soon as their feet touched the water, the river stopped flowing, and the waters piled up, creating a dry path for the people to cross! This miracle showed the Israelites and the nations around them that God was with Joshua, just as He had been with Moses at the Red Sea.

After everyone crossed, Joshua had one man from each tribe take a large stone from the riverbed and set them up as a memorial. Those stones were a reminder for future generations: "God made a way when there was no way." In the same way, we can remember our own "Jordan moments" by writing down how God has helped us and thanking Him, so we don't forget His faithfulness when new challenges come.

 ## ACTIVITY

Imagine walking on dry ground through a river in flood! How amazing would that be? Draw a river with a clear, dry path through the middle.

PRAYER

Powerful God, thank You for making a way where there seems to be no way. Help me to trust You to overcome obstacles in my life. Amen.

Chapter 163: The Fall of Jericho

"When the trumpets sounded, the army shouted, and at the sound of the trumpet, when the men gave a loud shout, the wall collapsed; so everyone charged straight in, and they took the city." - Joshua 6:20

The first city the Israelites faced in Canaan was Jericho, a strong city with high walls. God gave Joshua unusual instructions for taking the city. For six days, the army was to march around the city once a day, with priests blowing trumpets.

On the seventh day, they were to march around seven times, then the priests were to blow their trumpets, and all the people were to shout. When they obeyed, the walls of Jericho fell down flat! This showed that God fights for His people, and He wins battles in His own amazing way.

 **ACTIVITY**

Imagine shouting and watching a giant wall fall down. How incredible! Draw a simple wall with cracks or crumbling sections, representing the fall of Jericho.

PRAYER

Victorious God, thank You for fighting my battles. Help me to trust Your plans, even when they seem unusual, and to obey You completely. Amen.

Chapter 164: God Fights for Us

"The Lord will fight for you; you need only to be still." - Exodus 14:14

The story of Jericho clearly shows that God fights for His people. The Israelites did not win the battle by their own strength or cleverness. God gave them the victory. When we face big challenges or "battles" in our lives, we can remember that God is fighting for us. We do not have to be afraid or try to do everything in our own strength. We can trust God to be our defender and our champion.

At Jericho, God's plan looked unusual: march around the city for six days with the priests and the Ark, then circle it seven times on the seventh day, blow the trumpets, and shout. When they obeyed, the walls collapsed and the victory was clear. In the same way, God may lead us with simple steps of obedience, pray, keep going, do what's right, even when it doesn't make sense at first. He honors trust, and He knows how to bring walls down.

 **ACTIVITY**

Think about a time you felt someone was on your side, helping you in a difficult situation. How did that feel? Draw a simple shield with a cross on it, representing God fighting for us.

PRAYER

Fighting God, thank You for being my defender and fighting for me. Help me to trust in Your power and to be still, knowing You are in control. Amen.

Chapter 165: Dividing the Land

"So the Lord gave Israel all the land he had sworn to give their ancestors, and they took possession of it and settled there." - Joshua 21:43

After many battles, God helped the Israelites conquer the land of Canaan. Joshua then had the important task of dividing the land among the twelve tribes of Israel, just as God had promised. Each tribe received a portion of the land as their inheritance. This showed God's faithfulness to His promises made to Abraham, Isaac, and Jacob many years before. God always fulfills His word.

Joshua oversaw the division by lot before the Lord, making sure it was fair and orderly. The Levites didn't receive a large region like the other tribes; instead, they were given towns and pasturelands because their special inheritance was serving God. When the land was settled, God gave His people rest on every side, another clear sign that not one of His good promises had failed.

 # ACTIVITY

Imagine dividing a large pizza or cake fairly among many friends. How would you make sure everyone gets a piece? Draw a simple map with different sections, representing the divided land.

PRAYER

Faithful God, thank You for fulfilling Your promises. Help me to trust that You will always keep Your word and that You have a good inheritance for me. Amen.

Chapter 166: Choosing to Serve God

"But if serving the Lord seems undesirable to you, then choose for yourselves this day whom you will serve, whether the gods your ancestors served beyond the Euphrates, or the gods of the Amorites, in whose land you are living. But as for me and my household, we will serve the Lord." - Joshua 24:15

At the end of his life, Joshua gathered the Israelites and challenged them to choose whom they would serve. He reminded them of all God had done for them and urged them to serve the Lord with all their heart. Joshua declared, "As for me and my household, we will serve the Lord." This was a clear call to commitment. We also have a choice every day: will we serve God or something else?

A good way to answer that call is with simple, daily choices: put away

---

anything that pulls your heart from God, thank Him for His past help, and decide with your family what serving God looks like at home: how you speak, share, forgive, and tell the truth. Like Joshua's "household" promise, let your words become a pattern you live by, one faithful step at a time.

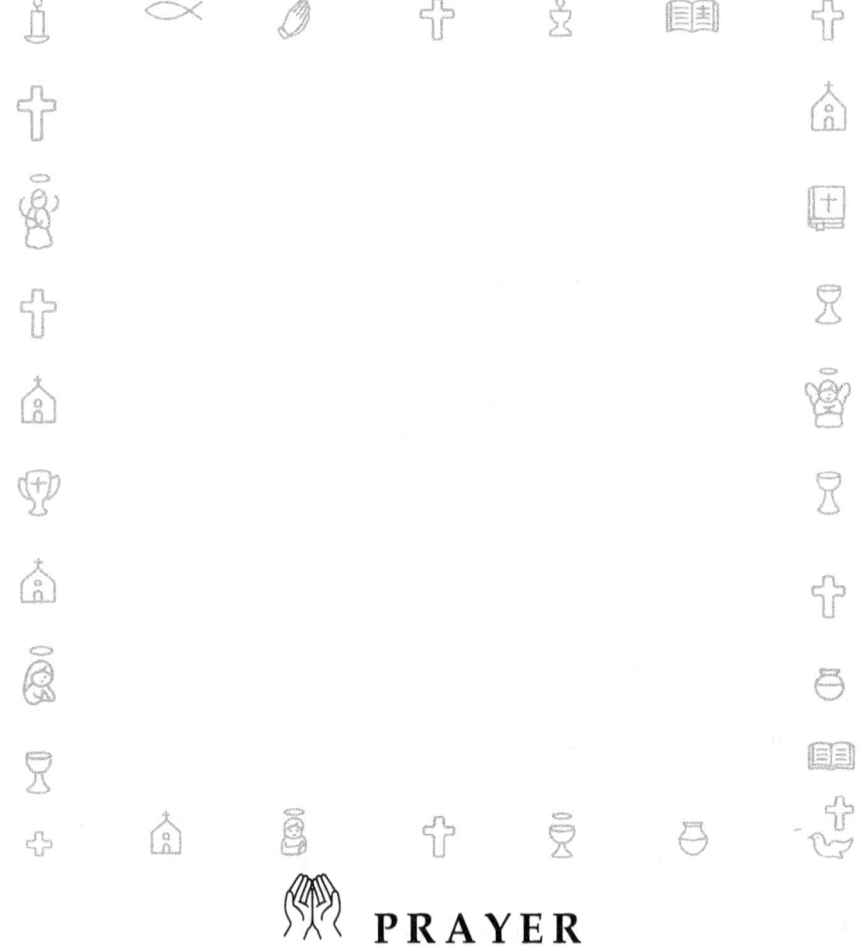

ACTIVITY

Think about a big choice you have to make. How do you decide? Draw a simple "fork in the road" with two paths, representing a choice.

PRAYER

God, thank You for giving me the choice to serve You. Help me to choose You every day and to serve You with all my heart, like Joshua. Amen.

Chapter 167: Deborah, a Brave Judge

"Now Deborah, a prophet, the wife of Lappidoth, was leading Israel at that time. She held court under the Palm of Deborah between Ramah and Bethel in the hill country of Ephraim, and the Israelites went up to her to have their disputes decided." - Judges 4:4-5

After Joshua, the Israelites sometimes forgot God and faced trouble. God raised up leaders called judges to rescue them. One of these judges was a brave woman named Deborah. She was a prophet, meaning God spoke through her, and she also judged disputes among the people. When the Israelites were oppressed by an enemy, God used Deborah to lead them to victory. She was a strong and courageous leader who trusted God completely.

Deborah called Barak to gather the army because God had promised to defeat Sisera, the enemy commander. Barak asked Deborah to go with him, and she did, reminding him that the honor for the victory would go to a woman. God kept His word: the enemy was defeated, and Jael finished the battle by stopping Sisera. Afterward, Deborah led the people in a song of praise, showing that true leadership listens to God, encourages others to obey, and gives Him the credit for every victory.

ACTIVITY

Think about a woman you know who is a strong leader or very brave. What makes them brave? Draw a simple figure of a woman standing tall, representing Deborah.

PRAYER

God, thank You for brave leaders like Deborah. Help me to be courageous and to trust You to lead me, no matter what. Amen.

Chapter 168: Gideon's Small Army

"The Lord said to Gideon, 'With the three hundred men that lapped, I will save you and give the Midianites into your hands. Let all the others go home.'" - Judges 7:7

The Israelites were again oppressed by an enemy, the Midianites. God called a man named Gideon to save them. Gideon felt weak and unsure. God told him to gather an army, but then God kept making the army smaller and smaller, until there were only 300 men! This was so that the Israelites would know the victory came from God, not from their own strength. Gideon obeyed, even though it seemed impossible.

ACTIVITY

Imagine being in a competition with only a few people on your team against a very large team. How would you feel? Draw a small group of people facing a large group, but with a shining light from above.

PRAYER

Powerful God, thank You for showing Your strength through weakness. Help me to trust You, even when I feel small or outnumbered. Amen.

Chapter 169: God's Strength, Not Ours

"So he said to me, "This is the word of the Lord to Zerubbabel: 'Not by might nor by power, but by my Spirit,' says the Lord Almighty." -Zechariah 4:6

Gideon's victory with only 300 men against a huge army showed a clear truth: the victory belonged to God. It was God's strength, not human strength, that won the battle. When we rely on God's strength, we can do amazing things. We do not have to be the strongest, the smartest, or the most talented. We just need to be willing to obey God, and He will provide the power.

 **ACTIVITY**

Think about something you accomplished that you could not have done alone. Who helped you? Draw a simple picture of a hand lifting something heavy, with another hand helping it.

PRAYER

God, thank You for Your strength that works through me. Help me to rely on You and to give You all the glory for what I accomplish. Amen.

Chapter 170: Samson's Strength

"Then the Spirit of the Lord came powerfully upon him so that he tore the lion apart with his bare hands as he might have torn a young goat." - Judges 14:6

Samson was another judge God raised up. God gave Samson incredible physical strength, but it was a special strength that came from God and was tied to a promise he made to God. Samson used his strength to fight against the Philistines, who were oppressing Israel. However, Samson often made poor choices and did not always use his strength wisely. This story reminds us that even with great gifts from God, we need to obey Him and use our gifts for His purposes.

 **ACTIVITY**

Think about a special talent or strength you have. How can you use it for good? Draw a simple figure with exaggerated strong arms.

PRAYER

God, thank You for the gifts and strengths You give me. Help me to use them wisely and for Your glory, always obeying Your will. Amen.

Chapter 171: Ruth's Loyalty

"But Ruth replied, 'Don't urge me to leave you or to turn back from following you. Where you go I will go, and where you stay I will stay. Your people will be my people and your God my God.'" - Ruth 1:16

After a famine, a woman named Naomi lost her husband and two sons. Her daughter-in-law, Ruth, chose to stay with Naomi, even though Naomi told her to go back to her own family. Ruth said, "Where you go I will go, and where you stay I will stay. Your people will be my people and your God my God." This shows amazing loyalty and love. Ruth chose to follow Naomi and to follow God. Her loyalty was a beautiful example of true devotion.

 **ACTIVITY**

Think about people you are loyal to, like your family or best friends. What does it mean to be loyal to them? Write their names on separate strips of paper. Link the strips together with tape or glue to create a "Loyalty Chain," symbolizing how you are connected.

_____

_____

_____

_____

_____

_____

_____

_____

_____

_____

PRAYER

God, thank You for showing me what loyalty means through Ruth. Help me to be loyal to You and to the people You have placed in my life. Amen.

Chapter 172: God's Care for Ruth

"Then Boaz said to Ruth, 'My daughter, listen to me. Don't go and glean in another field or leave this one. Stay here with my female servants.'" - Ruth 2:8

Ruth and Naomi were very poor when they arrived in Bethlehem. Ruth went to glean grain in the fields, picking up what the harvesters left behind. God showed His care for Ruth by leading her to the field of a kind man named Boaz.

Boaz was a relative of Naomi's husband, and he showed great kindness to Ruth, allowing her to gather plenty of grain. God provided for Ruth and Naomi through Boaz's generosity. This shows God's loving care for those who trust Him.

 **ACTIVITY**

God often provides for us in unexpected ways. Hide a few small, positive notes (e.g., "You are loved!", "God is good!") around a room for a family member to find. This is a "Hidden Blessings Hunt," reminding you that God's blessings are all around.

 **PRAYER**

Caring God, thank You for watching over me and providing for my needs. Help me to see Your blessings every day and to be grateful. Amen.

Chapter 173: Hannah's Prayer

"In her deep anguish Hannah prayed to the Lord, weeping bitterly." - 1 Samuel 1:10

In the time of the judges, there was a woman named Hannah who desperately wanted a child, but she could not have one. She was very sad and prayed to God with all her heart at the Tabernacle.

She promised God that if He gave her a son, she would dedicate him to God's service. God heard Hannah's prayer and answered it. This story shows that God listens to our deepest desires and answers prayers in His perfect timing.

 ## ACTIVITY

Think about something you really want to pray for. Decorate a small jar or container to be your "Prayer Jar." Write your prayer request on a small piece of paper and put it inside. You can add more prayers as you think of them.

 ## PRAYER

Listening God, thank You for hearing my prayers. Help me to pray with a sincere heart and to trust Your answers. Amen.

Chapter 174: Samuel Hears God's Voice

"Then the Lord came and stood there, calling as at the other times, 'Samuel! Samuel!' Then Samuel said, 'Speak, for your servant is listening.'" - 1 Samuel 3:10

Hannah kept her promise, and when her son Samuel was old enough, she took him to live and serve with the priest Eli at the Tabernacle. One night, while Samuel was sleeping, he heard a voice call his name. He thought it was Eli. After a few times, Eli realized it was God calling Samuel.

Eli told Samuel to answer, "Speak, Lord, for your servant is listening." Samuel listened, and God began to speak to him. This shows how important it is to listen carefully for God's voice.

 **ACTIVITY**

Play a simple game of "Whisper Challenge" or "Telephone" with a family member. One person whispers a message, and the next person repeats it. See how well the message travels. This helps you practice listening carefully, just like Samuel listened for God's voice.

PRAYER

Listening God, help me to hear Your voice when You speak. Open my ears and my heart to understand Your messages for me. Amen.

Chapter 175: God Chooses a King (Saul)

"Then Samuel took a flask of olive oil and poured it on Saul's head and kissed him, saying, "Has not the Lord anointed you ruler over his inheritance?" - 1 Samuel 10:1

The Israelites later wanted a king like the other nations. God told Samuel to anoint a man named Saul as their first king. Saul was from a small tribe and seemed like an unlikely choice. He was tall and handsome, but he was also humble at first. God chose him and gave him a new heart to lead His people.

This shows that God often chooses ordinary people for extraordinary tasks, and He looks at the heart.

 **ACTIVITY**

What qualities do you think make a good leader? Decorate a simple paper crown. As you decorate it, think about what kind of leader you would want to be, or what qualities you admire in a leader.

PRAYER

God, thank You for choosing leaders. Help me to see people as You see them and to remember that You can use anyone for Your purposes. Amen.

Chapter 176: David, a Shepherd Boy

"But the Lord said to Samuel, 'Do not consider his appearance or his height, for I have rejected him. The Lord does not look at the things people look at. People look at the outward appearance, but the Lord looks at the heart.'" - 1 Samuel 16:7

Saul eventually disobeyed God, and God decided to choose a new king. God sent Samuel to the house of Jesse to anoint one of his sons. Jesse presented his strong, older sons, but God told Samuel, "The Lord does not look at the things people look at. People look at the outward appearance, but the Lord looks at the heart." God chose the youngest son, David, a humble shepherd boy. David spent his days caring for sheep, but he also fought off lions and bears, showing his courage and skill.

 **ACTIVITY**

Find a stick outside or use a broom handle. Decorate it with ribbons or drawings to look like a shepherd's staff. As you do, think about how shepherds care for their sheep and how God cares for us, His flock.

PRAYER

God, thank You for looking at my heart. Help me to have a heart that loves and obeys You. Thank You for caring for me like a good shepherd. Amen.

Chapter 177: David and Goliath

"David said to the Philistine, 'You come against me with sword and spear and javelin, but I come against you in the name of the Lord Almighty, the God of the armies of Israel, whom you have defied.'" - 1 Samuel 17:45

The Philistines, Israel's enemies, had a giant warrior named Goliath, who was over nine feet tall! He challenged anyone from Israel to fight him, but everyone was terrified. David, the young shepherd boy, was not afraid. He trusted God. David went to fight Goliath with only a sling and five smooth stones. He told Goliath that he came against him in the name of the Lord Almighty. David slung a stone, hit Goliath in the forehead, and the giant fell! This was an amazing victory for God.

 ## ACTIVITY

Find a safe, open space. Use a soft ball or crumpled paper and try to hit a target (like a bucket or a drawn circle on the ground) from a few steps away. This is your "Target Practice" to remind you that even small things can have a big impact when God is with you.

 ## PRAYER

Brave God, thank You for giving David courage. Help me to be brave when I face big challenges and to trust in Your name. Amen.

Chapter 178: Courage in God

"Be strong and take heart, all you who hope in the Lord." - Psalm 31:24

David's courage against Goliath did not come from his own strength or size. It came from his trust in God. He knew God was bigger than any giant. True courage comes from knowing that God is with us and that He is more powerful than any problem we face. When we rely on God, we can be brave and do things we never thought possible.

 **ACTIVITY**

Draw a shield on a piece of paper. On the shield, write or draw symbols of things that give you courage because of God (e.g., a cross, a Bible, a happy face). This is your "Courage Shield."

 **PRAYER**

Courageous God, thank You for giving me strength and courage. Help me to trust in You and to be brave in every situation. Amen.

Chapter 179: David Becomes King

"Then all the tribes of Israel came to David at Hebron and said, 'We are your own flesh and blood. In the past, while Saul was king over us, you were the one who led Israel on their military campaigns. And the Lord said to you, "You will shepherd my people Israel, and you will be their ruler."'" - 2 Samuel 5:1-2

After defeating Goliath, David became a hero. He served King Saul, but Saul became jealous and tried to kill David many times. David had to run and hide, but he never tried to harm Saul, because Saul was God's anointed king. After Saul died, David eventually became king over all of Israel, just as God had planned. It was a long and difficult journey, but God was faithful to His promise.

 **ACTIVITY**

Think about a leader you admire. What qualities do they have? Brainstorm a list of "Leadership Qualities" (e.g., honest, kind, brave, good listener) and discuss how David showed some of these.

PRAYER

Faithful God, thank You for keeping Your promises, even through difficult times. Help me to be patient and to trust Your timing for my life. Amen.

Chapter 180: David's Heart for God

"After removing Saul, he made David their king. God testified concerning him: 'I have found David son of Jesse, a man after my own heart; he will do everything I want him to do.'" - Acts 13:22

David was known as a "man after God's own heart." This does not mean David was perfect. He made many mistakes. It means that David deeply loved God, sought to obey Him, and always returned to God when he sinned. David wrote many psalms, which are songs and prayers, showing his honest feelings to God. His heart was truly devoted to God.

We see this in his life: he trusted God to face Goliath, showed mercy to King Saul when he could have taken revenge, and confessed his sins honestly, asking God to forgive and change him. David teaches us to bring everything to God, our courage, our fears, our failures, and to keep coming back with a humble heart that wants to listen, obey, and worship.

 **ACTIVITY**

Draw a large heart on a piece of paper. Inside the heart, write or draw pictures of things you love and care about. Make sure to put God at the very center of your heart map, showing He is most important.

PRAYER

Loving God, thank You for David's example of a heart devoted to You. Help me to love You with all my heart and to always turn back to You when I make mistakes. Amen.

Chapter 181: King Solomon's Wisdom

"So give your servant a discerning heart to govern your people and to distinguish between right and wrong. For who is able to govern this great people of yours?" - 1 Kings 3:9

David's son, Solomon, became king after him. God appeared to Solomon in a dream and told him to ask for anything he wanted. Instead of asking for riches or a long life, Solomon asked for wisdom to govern God's people well. God was pleased with Solomon's request and gave him great wisdom, more than anyone else.

God also gave him riches and honor because he asked for wisdom first. This shows that God delights in giving us wisdom when we seek Him.

ACTIVITY

Write a simple riddle or puzzle for a family member to solve, or try to solve one they give you. As you do, discuss how wisdom helps us solve problems and make good choices.

PRAYER

Wise God, thank You for giving wisdom to Solomon. Please give me a discerning heart to make good choices and to understand Your ways. Amen.

Chapter 182: Building the Temple

"The house that King Solomon built for the Lord was sixty cubits long, twenty cubits wide and thirty cubits high." - 1 Kings 6:2

David had wanted to build a permanent house for God, a beautiful temple, but God told him his son, Solomon, would build it. Solomon used his wisdom and the vast resources God provided to build a magnificent Temple in Jerusalem. It was a grand building, a place where God's presence would dwell among His people. Building the Temple showed the Israelites' devotion to God and provided a central place for worship.

When the Temple was finished, the priests brought the Ark of the Covenant inside, and a cloud filled the building as a sign of God's glory. Solomon prayed, praising God for keeping His promises and asking Him to hear the prayers of His people. The Temple reminded everyone that God was near and faithful, yet greater than any building, calling them to worship Him with humble hearts and obedient lives.

 **ACTIVITY**

Using building blocks, LEGOs, or even pillows, try to build a small "special place" for worship.

 **PRAYER**

God, thank You for the desire to build places of worship. Help me to remember that my heart can be a special place for You to dwell. Amen.

Chapter 183: Elijah and the Prophets of Baal

"Elijah went before the people and said, 'How long will you waver between two opinions? If the Lord is God, follow him; but if Baal is God, follow him.' But the people said nothing." - 1 Kings 18:21

After Solomon, many kings in Israel led the people away from God to worship false gods like Baal. God sent a prophet named Elijah to challenge the prophets of Baal. Elijah proposed a contest: whichever god answered by fire would be the true God. The prophets of Baal cried out to their god all day, but nothing happened. Elijah then prayed to God.

 **ACTIVITY**

Write down a few simple statements, some true and some false (e.g., "The sky is green," "Dogs bark"). Read them aloud and sort them into "True" and "False" piles. This is your "Truth vs. Lie Sort," reminding you to choose the truth.

PRAYER

True God, thank You for showing us who You are. Help me to always follow You and to know the difference between truth and lies. Amen.

Chapter 184: God Sends Fire

"Then the fire of the Lord fell and burned up the sacrifice, the wood, the stones and the soil, and also licked up the water in the trench." - 1 Kings 18:38

After the prophets of Baal failed, Elijah rebuilt an altar to the Lord, placed a sacrifice on it, and poured water over it three times. Then he prayed a simple prayer, asking God to show that He was the true God. Immediately, fire fell from heaven! It consumed the sacrifice, the wood, the stones, the dust, and even licked up the water in the trench.

The people fell down and cried, "The Lord—he is God! The Lord—he is God!" This was a powerful demonstration of God's unmatched power.

 ACTIVITY

With adult supervision, do a simple, safe science experiment that shows a surprising reaction, like mixing baking soda and vinegar to create a fizzy "volcano." Talk about how God's power is even more amazing and real.

 PRAYER

Powerful God, thank You for showing Your mighty power. Help me to always remember that You are the one true God, and nothing is too difficult for You. Amen.

Chapter 185: Elisha's Miracles

"He picked up the cloak that had fallen from Elijah and went back and stood on the bank of the Jordan. Then he took the cloak that had fallen from Elijah and struck the water with it. 'Where now is the Lord, the God of Elijah?' he asked. When he struck the water, it divided to the right and to the left, and he crossed over." - 2 Kings 2:13-14

After Elijah, his servant Elisha became a prophet. God gave Elisha a double portion of Elijah's spirit, and Elisha performed many miracles. He healed the sick, multiplied food, and even raised a dead boy back to life. Elisha's miracles showed God's compassion and His power to bring life and healing. God continued to work through His prophets to care for His people.

 **ACTIVITY**

Perform one small, unexpected act of kindness for someone today. It could be helping with a chore, sharing a toy, or saying a kind word. Think about how these small acts can be like "mini-miracles" of kindness.

 **PRAYER**

Miraculous God, thank You for Your power to heal and provide. Help me to be Your hands and feet, showing kindness and helping others in need. Amen.

Chapter 186: Naaman Is Healed

"So Naaman went down and dipped himself in the Jordan seven times, as the man of God had told him, and his flesh was restored and became clean like that of a young boy." - 2 Kings 5:14

Naaman was a powerful army commander, but he had leprosy, a terrible skin disease. A young Israelite slave girl told Naaman's wife that a prophet in Israel could heal him. Naaman went to Elisha, who told him to dip seven times in the Jordan River. Naaman was angry because he expected something grander.

His servants convinced him to obey. He dipped seven times, and his skin was completely healed! This shows that God's ways are simple, and obedience, even when it seems strange, brings blessings.

 ## ACTIVITY

With a trusted adult, try a very gentle, short "trust fall" onto a soft surface (like a bed or couch). Or simply discuss what it means to trust someone's instructions, even if they seem unusual.

 ## PRAYER

Healing God, thank You for Your power to heal. Help me to be humble and to obey Your instructions, even when they seem simple or strange. Amen.

Chapter 187: Queen Esther's Courage

"Go, gather together all the Jews who are in Susa, and fast for me. Do not eat or drink for three days, night or day. I and my attendants will fast as you do. When this is done, I will go to the king, even though it is against the law. And if I perish, I perish." - Esther 4:16

Many years later, during the time of the Persian Empire, a Jewish orphan girl named Esther became queen. A wicked man named Haman planned to destroy all the Jewish people in the empire. Esther's cousin, Mordecai, urged her to speak to the king, even though it was dangerous. It was against the law to approach the king without being called, and it could mean death. Esther bravely decided to risk her life to save her people.

ACTIVITY

Draw a picture of Queen Esther. Around her, write down words that describe her bravery, like "brave," "selfless," "trusting God," or "determined." This is your "Courageous Character Sketch."

PRAYER

Brave God, thank You for giving Esther courage. Help me to be brave and to stand up for what is right, even when it is difficult or scary. Amen.

Chapter 188: Saving Her People

"For if you remain silent at this time, relief and deliverance for the Jews will arise from another place, but you and your father's family will perish. And who knows but that you have come to your royal position for such a time as this?" - Esther 4:14

Esther asked all the Jews to fast and pray for three days. Then, she bravely went to the king. The king welcomed her, and she invited him and Haman to two banquets. At the second banquet, Esther revealed Haman's evil plan to destroy her people. The king was furious and had Haman executed. Esther's courage saved her people from destruction. This shows how God can use one person's bravery to bring about great deliverance.

ACTIVITY

Set up a line of dominoes and knock over the first one to see the chain reaction. Discuss how one brave action, like Esther's, can have a big impact and lead to many good things.

PRAYER

Delivering God, thank You for Esther's bravery and for saving Your people. Help me to be a person You can use to make a difference in the world. Amen.

Chapter 189: Nehemiah Rebuilds the Wall

"I replied, 'The God of heaven will give us success. We his servants will start rebuilding, but as for you, you have no share in Jerusalem or any claim or historic right to it.'" - Nehemiah 2:20

Many years after the Jews returned from exile, the walls of Jerusalem were still broken down, leaving the city vulnerable. Nehemiah, a Jewish official serving the Persian king, heard about this and was heartbroken. He prayed to God and asked the king for permission to go and rebuild the walls. The king agreed. Nehemiah traveled to Jerusalem and rallied the people to work together to rebuild the walls, despite many enemies trying to stop them.

ACTIVITY

Try to build a small wall or structure. As you build, think about the challenges Nehemiah and the people faced and how they overcame them to rebuild the wall.

PRAYER

Working God, thank You for inspiring Nehemiah to rebuild. Help me to be a part of building up good things in my community and for Your kingdom. Amen.

Chapter 190: Working Together for God

"So we rebuilt the wall till all of it reached half its height, for the people worked with all their heart." - Nehemiah 4:6

Rebuilding the walls of Jerusalem was a huge task, but Nehemiah organized the people so that everyone worked together. Each family or group was responsible for a section of the wall. They faced opposition, so they worked with one hand and held a weapon with the other.

Their teamwork and dedication, with God's help, allowed them to finish the wall in just 52 days! This shows how much can be accomplished when God's people work together for His purposes.

ACTIVITY

Work on a jigsaw puzzle with a family member or friend. As you put the pieces together, discuss how each person's contribution is important and how teamwork helps you achieve a goal.

PRAYER

Unifying God, thank You for showing me the power of working together. Help me to be a good team member and to work with others to accomplish Your will. Amen.

Chapter 191: Daniel in the Lion's Den

"My God sent his angel, and he shut the mouths of the lions. They have not hurt me, because I was found innocent in his sight. Nor have I ever done any wrong before you, Your Majesty." - Daniel 6:22

Daniel was a faithful man who served God in Babylon. Some jealous officials tricked the king into signing a law that said no one could pray to any god or person except the king for thirty days. Daniel knew this was wrong. He continued to pray to God three times a day, just as he always did. Because he disobeyed the king's law, he was thrown into a den of hungry lions. But God sent an angel to shut the lions' mouths, and Daniel was unharmed!

 ## ACTIVITY

Create a simple lion mask using a paper plate, string, and markers. As you make it, think about how Daniel was brave even when facing danger.

 ## PRAYER

Protecting God, thank You for protecting Daniel. Help me to be faithful to You, even when it is difficult, and to trust that You will watch over me. Amen.

Chapter 192: Trusting God in Danger

"The Lord is my light and my salvation—whom shall I fear? The Lord is the stronghold of my life—of whom shall I be afraid?" - Psalm 27:1

Daniel faced extreme danger, but he trusted God completely. He knew that God was powerful enough to save him, even from hungry lions. Daniel's trust in God meant he was not afraid to do what was right, even if it meant risking his life. When we face danger or scary situations, we can trust God to be with us and to protect us. His presence gives us peace.

 **ACTIVITY**

Draw a picture of your "safe place," real or imagined. Think about how God is always your safest place, no matter what dangers you face.

PRAYER

Trustworthy God, thank You for being my refuge and strength in danger. Help me to trust You completely and to feel Your peace when I am afraid. Amen.

Chapter 193: Shadrach, Meshach, and Abednego

"But even if he does not, we want you to know, Your Majesty, that we will not serve your gods or worship the image of gold you have set up." - Daniel 3:18

In Babylon, three of Daniel's friends, Shadrach, Meshach, and Abednego, also served God faithfully. King Nebuchadnezzar made a giant gold statue and commanded everyone to bow down and worship it. If they refused, they would be thrown into a blazing furnace.

Shadrach, Meshach, and Abednego refused to bow down. They told the king that their God was able to save them, but even if He did not, they would still not worship the idol. This shows amazing courage and devotion to God.

 ## ACTIVITY

Stand up straight and tall. Think about something you believe in very strongly. Practice saying, "I believe..." and finish the sentence with something that is true about God. This helps you "stand tall" for your beliefs.

 ## PRAYER

Faithful God, thank You for the courage of Shadrach, Meshach, and Abednego. Help me to stand firm in my faith and to always choose to worship only You. Amen.

Chapter 194: God Delivers Them

"He said, 'Look! I see four men walking around in the fire, unbound and unharmed, and the fourth looks like a son of the gods.'" - Daniel 3:25

King Nebuchadnezzar was furious and ordered the furnace to be heated seven times hotter than usual. Shadrach, Meshach, and Abednego were thrown into the blazing fire. The king looked into the furnace and saw not three men, but four, and the fourth one looked like a son of the gods! The men walked around unharmed. When they came out, they did not even smell of smoke. God miraculously delivered them! This showed the king and everyone else that God is the only true God, who saves those who trust Him.

 **ACTIVITY**

Create a very simple "escape" challenge in a room. Hide a small reward and leave clues that lead to it. When you find the reward, talk about how God delivers us from difficult situations.

PRAYER

Delivering God, thank You for Your amazing power to save. Thank You for protecting Shadrach, Meshach, and Abednego. Help me to trust You to deliver me from my troubles. Amen.

Chapter 195: Jonah and the Big Fish

"But the Lord provided a great fish to swallow Jonah, and Jonah was in the belly of the fish three days and three nights." - Jonah 1:17

God told a prophet named Jonah to go to the great city of Nineveh and tell the people to turn from their wickedness. Jonah did not want to go. He tried to run away from God by getting on a ship going in the opposite direction. God sent a great storm, and the sailors threw Jonah overboard. God then sent a huge fish to swallow Jonah! Jonah was in the fish's belly for three days and three nights. This shows that we cannot run from God, and He will go to great lengths to get our attention.

 **ACTIVITY**

Make a simple fish craft using a paper plate, construction paper, and markers. As you make it, talk about how Jonah tried to run away from God's plan and how the big fish brought him back.

PRAYER

Pursuing God, thank You for always being with me, even when I try to run away. Help me to obey You and to follow Your plans for my life. Amen.

Chapter 196: God's Mercy for Nineveh

"When God saw what they did and how they turned from their evil ways, he relented and did not bring on them the destruction he had threatened." - Jonah 3:10

While inside the fish, Jonah prayed to God, and God commanded the fish to spit Jonah out onto dry land. God told Jonah again to go to Nineveh. This time, Jonah obeyed. He preached to the people of Nineveh, telling them that God would destroy their city because of their wickedness. The people of Nineveh believed God, repented, and turned from their evil ways. God saw their changed hearts and showed them mercy, not destroying their city. This shows God's incredible compassion and His willingness to forgive when people turn to Him.

 **ACTIVITY**

Think of someone who might need a little extra kindness today. Plan a small "mercy mission" for them, like drawing them a card, sharing a snack, or offering to help with a small chore.

PRAYER

Merciful God, thank You for Your great compassion and for forgiving those who turn to You. Help me to be merciful to others, just as You are to me. Amen.

Chapter 197: Prophets Speak God's Word

"Surely the Sovereign Lord does nothing without revealing his plan to his servants the prophets." - Amos 3:7

Elijah, Elisha, Jonah, and many others were prophets in the Old Testament. A prophet was someone God chose to speak His messages to people. They delivered God's warnings, His promises, and His instructions. Sometimes the messages were difficult, and sometimes people did not want to listen. Prophets were brave and faithful to speak what God told them, even when it was unpopular.

Often God confirmed their words with signs or special actions, fire on Mount Carmel, a widow's oil that didn't run out, a great fish that turned Jonah back toward Nineveh. The heart of their work wasn't performing miracles; it was calling people to turn from wrong and return to God.

Their courage came from listening to God first, then speaking with honesty and love, an example for us to follow when we need to stand for what is right.

ACTIVITY

Play a game of "Message Relay." One person whispers a secret message to another, who then whispers it to the next, and so on. The last person says the message aloud. Discuss how prophets were like messengers for God.

PRAYER

Speaking God, thank You for speaking to us through Your Word and through Your messengers. Help me to listen carefully to Your messages and to share Your truth with others. Amen.

Chapter 198: Isaiah's Message of Hope

"For to us a child is born, to us a son is given, and the government will be on his shoulders. And he will be called Wonderful Counselor, Mighty God, Everlasting Father, Prince of Peace." - Isaiah 9:6

Isaiah was a prophet who lived hundreds of years before Jesus was born. He spoke many warnings to the people of Israel because of their sin, but he also spoke powerful messages of hope. Isaiah prophesied about the coming of a Savior, Jesus, who would be born of a virgin, would suffer for our sins, and would bring peace and light to the world. His messages gave people hope for a future with God.

Isaiah painted hope with vivid pictures: a great light shining on people walking in darkness, a child who would be a wise and just ruler, a faithful servant who would carry our wrongs, and even a world at peace where former enemies live safely together. He also reminded everyone that human strength fades like grass, but God's word stands forever. These promises help us trust God's heart, even when times are hard, because He keeps what He says and works out His rescue plan in His perfect time.

 **ACTIVITY**

Cut out pictures from old magazines or draw simple symbols that represent hope (e.g., a sunrise, a seedling, a smiling face). Create a small "Hope Collage" on a piece of paper.

PRAYER

God of Hope, thank You for sending prophets like Isaiah to bring messages of hope. Thank You for the promise of Jesus, our Prince of Peace. Amen.

Chapter 199: Jeremiah's Call

"Before I formed you in the womb I knew you, before you were born I set you apart; I appointed you as a prophet to the nations." - Jeremiah 1:5

Jeremiah was another prophet God called. God told Jeremiah that He knew him before he was born and had chosen him to be a prophet to the nations. Jeremiah felt very young and said he did not know how to speak. God touched Jeremiah's mouth and put His words in it, promising to be with him. Jeremiah faced many difficult times because people did not want to hear his messages, but he remained faithful to God's call.

Even when he was mocked, threatened, or felt like giving up, Jeremiah kept speaking the truth with a tender heart for his people. His life reminds us that courage isn't the absence of fear: it's choosing to obey God and love others even when it's hard.

 ACTIVITY

Practice speaking clearly and confidently about something you believe in. It could be your favorite animal, why it is important to be kind, or something you learned about God today. This helps you be a "Brave Speaker."

 PRAYER

Calling God, thank You for knowing me and for having a plan for my life. Help me to be brave and to speak Your truth, even when it is difficult. Amen.

Chapter 200: Trusting God's Plan

"Many are the plans in a person's heart, but it is the Lord's purpose that prevails." - Proverbs 19:21

We have explored many stories of brave hearts in the Old Testament: Noah, Abraham, Joseph, Moses, Joshua, Deborah, Gideon, Ruth, Hannah, Samuel, David, Solomon, Elijah, Elisha, Esther, Nehemiah, Daniel, and Jonah. Through all their adventures and challenges, God was working out His perfect plan. He used ordinary people to do extraordinary things.

This reminds us that God has a big plan for history and for each of our lives. We can trust His plan, even when we do not understand every step.

ACTIVITY

Write down the names of 5-7 key people from the stories in Part 2 on separate strips of paper. Link them together in order (e.g., Noah, Abraham, Joseph, Moses, Joshua, David, Esther). This is your "Story Chain," showing how God connected all their lives in His big plan.

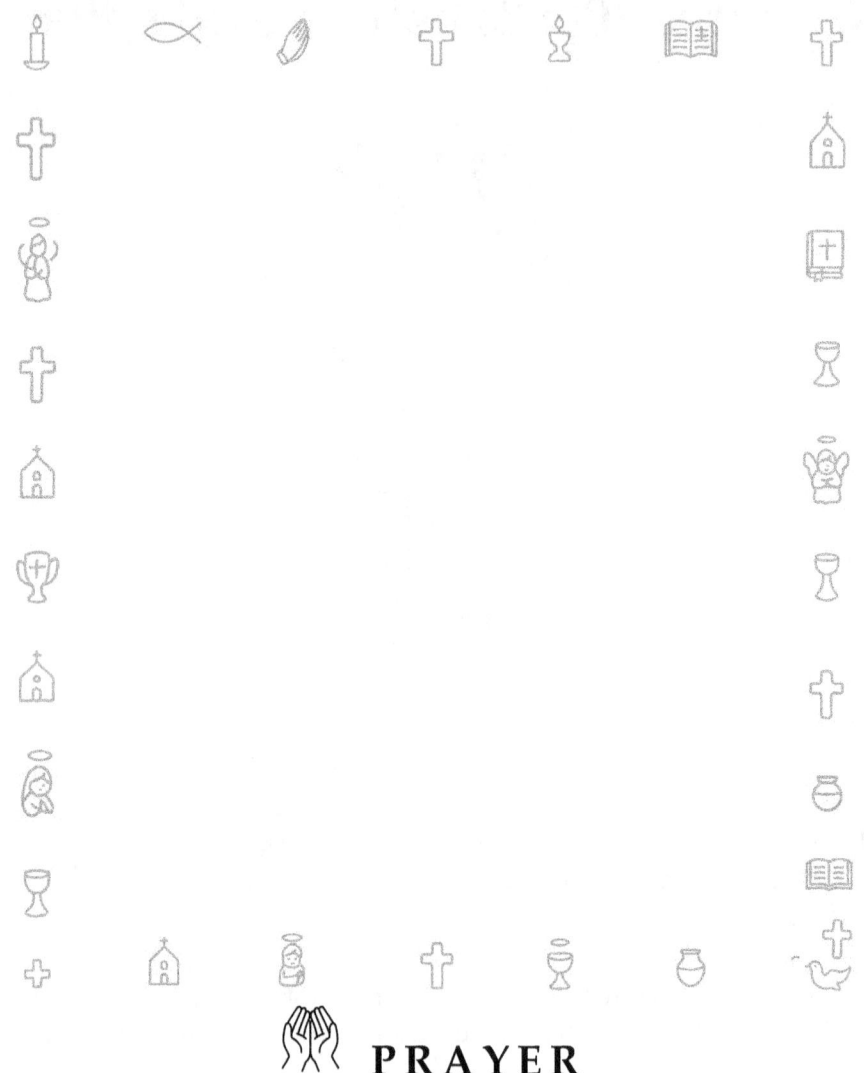

PRAYER

God of all plans, thank You for Your amazing purpose that prevails through history. Help me to trust Your plan for my life and to live for Your glory. Amen.

Chapter 201: God's Strength in Weakness

"But he said to me, 'My grace is sufficient for you, for my power is made perfect in weakness.' Therefore I will boast all the more gladly about my weaknesses, so that Christ's power may rest on me." - 2 Corinthians 12:9

Many of the brave people in the Bible, like Gideon and Jeremiah, felt weak or unable to do what God asked. God showed that His strength is made perfect in their weakness. When we feel too small, not smart enough, or not strong enough, that is when God's power can truly shine through us. We do not need to rely on our own abilities; we can rely on God's limitless strength to help us.

 **ACTIVITY**

Try to lift something that is a little too heavy for you on your own (like a small box of books). Then, ask an adult to help you lift it. This "Team Lift" activity reminds you that with help, especially God's, even heavy burdens can be moved.

 **PRAYER**

Strong God, thank You for being powerful when I feel weak. Help me to remember that Your strength is enough for me, and to lean on You in every challenge. Amen.

Chapter 202: Standing Up for What Is Right

"Do not conform to the pattern of this world, but be transformed by the renewing of your mind. Then you will be able to test and approve what God's will is—his good, pleasing and perfect will." - Romans 12:2

Daniel and his friends, Shadrach, Meshach, and Abednego, showed incredible bravery by standing up for what was right, even when it meant facing a lion's den or a fiery furnace. They refused to compromise their faith in God. Standing up for what is right can be hard, especially when others are doing something wrong. God gives us courage to do the right thing, even when it is unpopular or scary.

Their courage grew from trusting God every day, praying regularly, choosing obedience in small things, and standing together as friends. When they refused to bow to an idol, God was with them in the fire;

when Daniel kept praying, God shut the lions' mouths. We can practice the same kind of courage by praying, doing what's right even when no one is watching, and finding friends who will stand with us. God is near, and He helps us be brave.

ACTIVITY

Write down a few common peer pressure situations (e.g., "Someone wants you to cheat on a test," "A friend wants you to say something mean about someone"). For each one, think of a brave and right way to respond. This is your "Brave Choices Scenario."

PRAYER

Righteous God, thank You for helping me know what is right. Give me the courage to stand up for Your truth, even when it is difficult. Amen.

Chapter 203: Leading with Humility

"He has shown you, O mortal, what is good. And what does the Lord require of you? To act justly and to love mercy and to walk humbly with your God." - Micah 6:8

Moses was a powerful leader, but he was also described as very humble. David, despite being a king, often humbled himself before God. True leaders serve others and give glory to God, not to themselves. Humility means recognizing that all our talents and positions come from God. When we lead with humility, we become better examples and more effective for God's kingdom.

You can practice humility in simple ways: listen before you speak, give credit to others, say "I'm sorry" when you're wrong, and look for quiet ways to help. Real leadership is about serving faithfully and pointing people's eyes to God.

 **ACTIVITY**

Think about a time you helped someone without expecting anything in return. How did that feel? Create a "Humility Helper" chart for a day, listing small acts of service you can do for family members without being asked.

PRAYER

Humble God, thank You for showing me what true leadership looks like. Help me to serve others with a humble heart and to always give You the glory. Amen.

Chapter 204: Serving Others

"Each of you should use whatever gift you have received to serve others, as faithful stewards of God's grace in its various forms." - 1 Peter 4:10

Many brave hearts in the Bible, from Joseph saving his family to Nehemiah rebuilding the wall, showed their love for God by serving others. Serving means putting the needs of others before our own. When we serve, we are following Jesus' example, who came not to be served, but to serve. Serving others is a practical way to show God's love in the world.

You can practice serving right where you are: look for one small need each day and meet it: share your lunch, include someone left out, help with chores before being asked, or pray for a friend who's having a hard time. Ask God each morning, "Who can I help today?" and be ready to act with a cheerful heart. Small acts done with big love make a real difference.

 **ACTIVITY**

Think about someone in your family or community who could use a little help. Plan a simple "Service Surprise" for them, like doing a chore they usually do, or making them a small card.

PRAYER

Serving God, thank You for the example of serving others. Help me to use my gifts to serve those around me and to show Your love. Amen.

Chapter 205: Being a Good Friend

"A friend loves at all times, and a brother is born for a time of adversity." -Proverbs 17:17

The Bible shows us the importance of good friends. David and Jonathan had a deep friendship, showing loyalty and sacrifice. Being a good friend means being kind, trustworthy, supportive, and forgiving. It means being there for others in good times and bad. Our friendships can be a reflection of God's love for us and how we should love one another.

Choose friends who encourage you to do what's right, and be that kind of friend to others. Keep your word, listen well, celebrate their wins, and forgive quickly when mistakes happen. Pray for your friends, include those who feel left out, and speak the truth with kindness. Strong, God-shaped friendships help us grow brave, wise, and joyful.

 **ACTIVITY**

Write a kind note or draw a picture for a friend or sibling. Give it to them as a "Friendship Booster" to let them know you appreciate them.

PRAYER

God, thank You for the gift of friendship. Help me to be a good and loyal friend, showing kindness and support to those around me. Amen.

Chapter 206: Speaking Truth in Love

"Instead, speaking the truth in love, we will grow to become in every respect the mature body of him who is the head, that is, Christ." - Ephesians 4:15

Prophets like Isaiah and Jeremiah had to speak difficult truths to the people, but they did it out of love for God and His people. Speaking truth in love means being honest, but also being kind and gentle with our words. It is not about hurting others, but about helping them. God wants us to be truthful, but also to be loving in how we communicate.

A helpful way to do this is to pause and pray before you speak, then choose words that build up rather than tear down. Ask questions, listen well, and share the truth calmly and clearly, aiming to help the person, not win an argument. When our tone is gentle and our heart is caring, hard truths can become healing truths.

 ACTIVITY

Practice saying something you need to say that might be difficult (e.g., "I need a turn," "I don't like that") using a kind and gentle voice. This is your "Kind Words Practice."

 PRAYER

God of Truth and Love, help me to speak the truth in a way that is kind and helpful. Guide my words so that they build up and do not tear down. Amen.

Chapter 207: Overcoming Fear

"For God has not given us a spirit of fear, but of power and of love and of a sound mind." - 2 Timothy 1:7

Many brave hearts in the Bible, like Joshua facing Jericho or Daniel in the lion's den, had to overcome fear. They did not let fear stop them from obeying God. Overcoming fear does not mean we never feel afraid. It means we choose to trust God and move forward even when we are scared. God gives us courage and promises to be with us, so we do not have to be controlled by fear.

When fear shows up, try this: pause and breathe, talk to God about what worries you, and take the next small step of obedience. Remember times He's helped you before, and ask a trusted adult or friend to stand with you. Courage grows one choice at a time, and each brave choice makes the next one easier.

 **ACTIVITY**

Write down one small fear you have (e.g., fear of a test, fear of trying something new). Then, write down one Bible verse or truth about God that helps you overcome that fear. This is your "Fear Fighter Verse."

_____

_____

_____

_____

_____

_____

_____

_____

_____

_____

PRAYER

Brave God, thank You for not giving me a spirit of fear. Fill me with Your power, love, and a sound mind to overcome my fears. Amen.

Chapter 208: God's Call for Us

"And we know that in all things God works for the good of those who love him, who have been called according to his purpose." - Romans 8:28

Just as God called Moses, Joshua, and many others for specific tasks, God has a call for each of us. He has a purpose for your life. This call might not be to lead a nation, but it could be to be a kind friend, a diligent student, or someone who shares God's love with others. When God calls us, He also gives us what we need to fulfill that call.

You can start by asking, "God, how can I serve You today?" Then look for small ways to obey: tell the truth, include someone left out, finish your work with excellence, or offer to help at home or church. As you take these simple steps, God guides your path and equips you with the courage, wisdom, and strength you need.

 # ACTIVITY

Create a "Purpose Map." Draw a circle in the middle with your name. Around it, draw or write down things you enjoy doing, things you are good at, and ways you can help others. Connect them with lines to show how God might use you.

PRAYER

Calling God, thank You for having a purpose for my life. Help me to understand Your call and to live each day in a way that fulfills Your good plan. Amen.

Chapter 209: Using Our Talents for God

"Each of you should use whatever gift you have received to serve others, as faithful stewards of God's grace in its various forms." - 1 Peter 4:10

God gave Samson great strength, Solomon great wisdom, and David musical talent. Each of these gifts was meant to be used for God's purposes. God has given each of us unique talents and abilities.

Whether you are good at drawing, singing, playing sports, solving math problems, or making people laugh, these are gifts from God. He wants us to use them to serve Him and to bless others.

 ACTIVITY

Create a "Talent Show" for your family. Share one of your talents (e.g., sing a song, show a drawing, tell a joke). After, talk about how you can use that talent to bring joy to others or honor God.

 **PRAYER**

Gift-Giving God, thank You for the talents You have given me. Help me to use my gifts to serve You and to bless the people around me. Amen.

Chapter 210: Being a Witness

"But you will receive power when the Holy Spirit comes on you; and you will be my witnesses in Jerusalem, and in all Judea and Samaria, and to the ends of the earth." - Acts 1:8

Many brave hearts in the Old Testament were witnesses for God. They showed others who God was through their lives and their words. Joseph was a witness in Egypt. Daniel was a witness in Babylon. Being a witness means showing and telling others about God's goodness, power, and love. Our lives can be a powerful testimony to what God can do.

You can be a witness right where you are: choose honesty when it's hard, show kindness to someone left out, and give God credit when He helps you. Pray for chances to share a simple "God story" from your life, how He answered a prayer or gave you courage, and let your actions and words point people toward Him.

 ## ACTIVITY

Think about one way you can show someone about God's love today without saying a word (e.g., a kind action, a helpful gesture). This is your "Silent Witness Challenge."

 ## PRAYER

Witnessing God, thank You for making me Your witness. Help me to show others Your love and truth through my actions and my words. Amen.

Chapter 211: God's Promises for the Future

"For I know the plans I have for you,' declares the Lord, 'plans to prosper you and not to harm you, plans to give you hope and a future.'" - *Jeremiah 29:11*

The prophets in the Old Testament, like Isaiah and Jeremiah, spoke many promises about the future, especially about the coming of the Messiah, Jesus. These promises gave people hope. God still has promises for our future, including eternal life with Him in heaven. These promises give us something wonderful to look forward to and help us live with hope and purpose today.

Because God keeps His word, we can wait with courage and live with purpose now, choosing honesty, kindness, and trust even when life feels uncertain. One simple practice is to write down a promise of God, thank

Him for it each day, and look for small ways He's already keeping it. Hope grows when we remember what He has said and take the next faithful step.

ACTIVITY

Draw a picture of what you imagine heaven might be like. Think about the promises God has made about our future with Him. This is your "Heavenly Hope Sketch."

PRAYER

God of Hope, thank You for Your wonderful promises for my future. Help me to live with hope and to look forward to the amazing things You have planned. Amen.

Chapter 212: God's Enduring Patience

"The Lord is not slow in keeping his promise, as some understand slowness. Instead he is patient with you, not wanting anyone to perish, but everyone to come to repentance." - 2 Peter 3:9

We have seen how God was incredibly patient with the Israelites, even when they complained and disobeyed Him over and over again. God's patience endures. It means He does not give up on us easily. He continues to teach us, guide us, and wait for us to turn back to Him. His enduring patience is a sign of His deep love.

When you feel like you've messed up, remember that God is still inviting you to start again. Talk to Him honestly, say you're sorry, and take the next right step. His patience is like an open door, always ready for you to walk back in and keep growing.

 **ACTIVITY**

Find a small plant or seed. Observe how it takes time to grow. This "Growth Observation" reminds you that growth takes patience, just as God is patient with us.

 **PRAYER**

Patient God, thank You for Your enduring patience with me. Help me to learn from my mistakes and to grow closer to You each day, knowing You never give up on me. Amen.

Chapter 213: God's Perfect Timing

"He has made everything beautiful in its time. He has also set eternity in the human heart; yet no one can fathom what God has done from beginning to end." - Ecclesiastias 3:11

From Joseph's rise to power to the fall of Jericho, God's perfect timing was evident. He knew exactly when to act. God's timing is always best, even if it does not match our own timeline. We can trust that He knows the right moment for everything in our lives, and His delays are not denials. Waiting on His perfect timing requires faith.

Think of it like a seed underground: nothing seems to be happening, but roots are growing where you can't see. While you wait, talk to God about your hopes, thank Him for past help, and do the next right thing today. In the right season, He brings the growth and opens the door you need.

 # ACTIVITY

Play a game where timing is important, like "Red Light, Green Light" or a simple clapping game with a rhythm. Talk about how important timing is in the game and how God's timing is perfect in life.

 # PRAYER

God of perfect timing, thank You for knowing the best moment for everything. Help me to trust Your timing and to wait patiently for Your plans to unfold. Amen.

Chapter 214: God's Unchanging Character

"Jesus Christ is the same yesterday and today and forever." - Hebrews 13:8

Through all the different stories and challenges in the Old Testament, God's character remained constant. He was always holy, just, loving, and faithful. God is unchanging. He is the same yesterday, today, and forever. This means we can always rely on Him to be who He says He is. His unchanging character gives us security and stability in a changing world.

 **ACTIVITY**

Find an object that is very strong and stable, like a large rock or a sturdy tree. Think about how it stays the same even when things around it change. Draw a picture of this strong, unchanging object.

PRAYER

Unchanging God, thank You for Your constant character. Help me to find my security in You and to always trust who You are. Amen.

Chapter 215: God's Goodness in All Things

"And we know that in all things God works for the good of those who love him, who have been called according to his purpose." - Romans 8:28

Even when bad things happened to Joseph, or when the Israelites faced difficulties, God was still good. He used those situations for good purposes. God's goodness is not dependent on our circumstances. He is inherently good, and He works all things for the good of those who love Him. We can always find evidence of God's goodness, even in challenging times.

 **ACTIVITY**

Create a "Goodness Jar." Throughout the day, write down small good things that happen or that you notice (e.g., "sunny weather," "a kind word," "a tasty snack"). Put them in the jar and review them at the end of the day to see God's goodness.

PRAYER

Good God, thank You for Your goodness that is present in all things. Help me to see Your hand working for good, even when things are difficult. Amen.

Chapter 216: God's Faithfulness to Generations

"Your faithfulness continues through all generations; you established the earth, and it endures." - Psalm 119:90

God made promises to Abraham, and He was faithful to those promises through Isaac, Jacob, Joseph, Moses, and Joshua, and all the generations that followed. God's faithfulness extends from one generation to the next. He is faithful to His people throughout history. This means God will be faithful to you and to future generations who love Him.

 **ACTIVITY**

Draw a simple family tree, including yourself, your parents, and your grandparents. Think about how God has been faithful to your family through the generations.

PRAYER

Faithful God, thank You for Your faithfulness that continues through all generations. Help me to be a part of Your faithful family and to pass on Your truth. Amen.

Chapter 217: God's Sovereignty in History

"The Lord does whatever pleases him, in the heavens and on the earth, in the seas and all their depths." - Psalm 135:6

The stories of the Old Testament show that God is sovereign over all of history. He controls kings, empires, and all events to bring about His purposes. He used Pharaoh, Cyrus, and many others to fulfill His plans. God's sovereignty means He is the ultimate ruler, and nothing happens without His knowledge or permission. We can trust that He is guiding history towards His perfect goal.

 ACTIVITY

Pick a historical event you know about (e.g., a famous invention, a past holiday). Think about how many different people and events had to come together for it to happen. Discuss how God orchestrates big events.

 PRAYER

Sovereign God, thank You for being in control of all history. Help me to trust Your rule and to know that You are working out Your purposes in the world. Amen.

Chapter 218: God's Love for All People

"The Lord is good to all; he has compassion on all he has made." - Psalm 145:9

While the Old Testament often focuses on God's chosen people, Israel, stories like Jonah going to Nineveh remind us that God's love is for all people. He desires all people to turn to Him and find forgiveness. God's love is not limited to one group; it extends to everyone on earth. This means God loves you, your friends, your neighbors, and people all around the world.

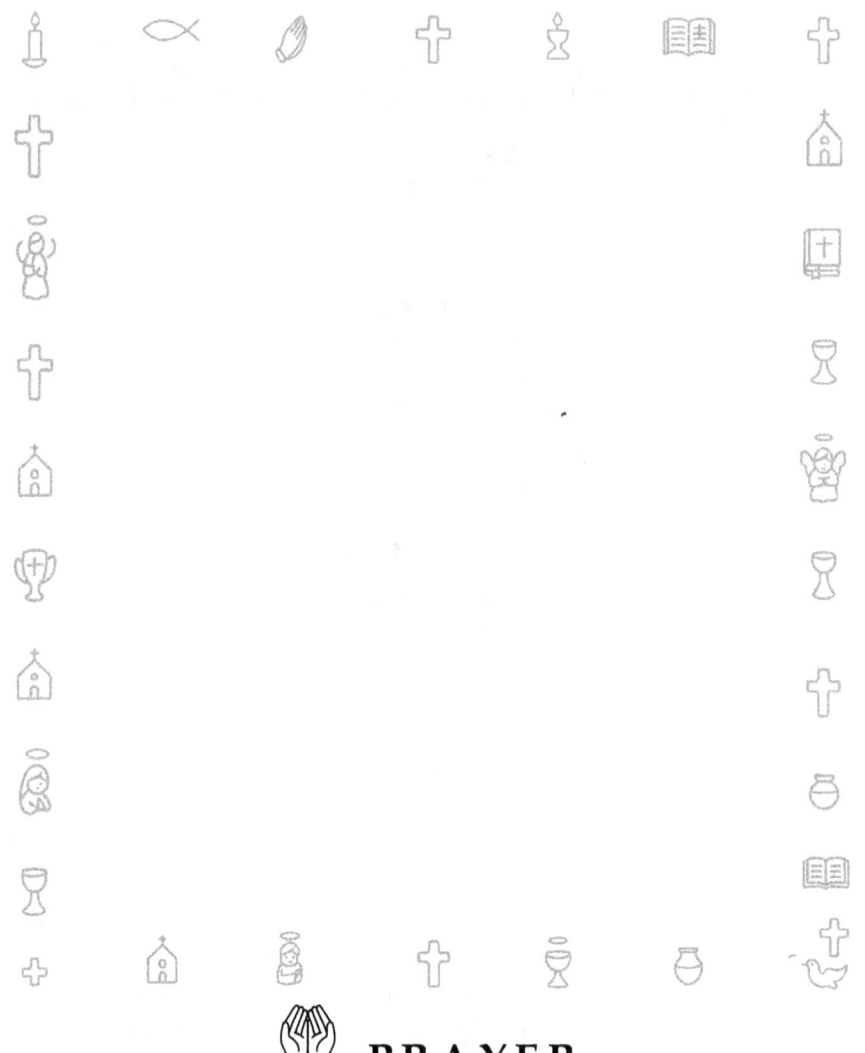 ACTIVITY

Draw a simple map of the world. On it, draw hearts in different places, representing God's love for all people everywhere.

PRAYER

Loving God, thank You for Your great love for all people. Help me to love others as You do and to share Your love with everyone I meet. Amen.

Chapter 219: God's Call to Obedience

"If you love me, keep my commands." - John 14:15

Throughout the Old Testament, God repeatedly called His people to obedience. He gave them laws and instructions because He loved them and wanted what was best for them. Obedience is a response of love and trust to God. When we obey God, we show that we trust His wisdom and that we want to please Him. It is a key part of having a close relationship with God.

ACTIVITY

Create a "Commandment Charades" game. Write down a few simple commands (e.g., "Clean your room," "Be kind," "Listen to your parents"). Act them out for a family member to guess. Discuss how obeying commands helps things go smoothly.

PRAYER

Obedient God, thank You for giving me Your commands. Help me to obey You with a joyful heart, knowing that my obedience shows my love for You. Amen.

Chapter 220: God's Amazing Love in Action

"But God demonstrates his own love for us in this: While we were still sinners, Christ died for us." - Romans 5:8

We have seen God's amazing love in action throughout the Old Testament: in creation, in saving Noah, in guiding Abraham, in providing for Joseph, in delivering Israel from Egypt, and in raising up brave leaders like David and Esther. God's love is not just a feeling; it is an active, powerful force that works in the world. His love is the foundation of everything He does.

 **ACTIVITY**

Think about the most amazing act of love you have ever seen or heard about. What made it so amazing? Draw a picture that represents God's amazing love in action, like a heart with hands helping someone.

PRAYER

Loving God, thank You for Your amazing love that is always in action. Help me to understand the depth of Your love and to share it with everyone I meet. Amen.

Chapter 221: A Long Wait for the Savior

"But when the set time had fully come, God sent his Son, born of a woman, born under the law." - Galatians 4:4

After the Old Testament stories, there was a long time, about 400 years, when God did not send any prophets to speak to His people. It might have felt like God was silent, but He was still working behind the scenes. During this time, people were waiting for the promised Savior, the Messiah, whom the prophets had spoken about. This long wait shows God's perfect timing and how He prepares the world for His biggest plan.

ACTIVITY

Imagine waiting for a very special birthday or holiday. How does the anticipation build? Draw a simple hourglass, representing the long period of waiting for the Savior.

PRAYER

Patient God, thank You for Your perfect timing. Help me to trust You even when I have to wait, knowing You are always working out Your good plans. Amen.

Chapter 222: Prophecies of Jesus

"For to us a child is born, to us a son is given, and the government will be on his shoulders. And he will be called Wonderful Counselor, Mighty God, Everlasting Father, Prince of Peace." - Isaiah 9:6

Hundreds of years before Jesus was born, prophets like Isaiah and Micah spoke many prophecies about Him. They said He would be born in Bethlehem, that He would be called Immanuel (meaning "God with us"), and that He would be a wonderful counselor and Prince of Peace. These prophecies showed God's amazing knowledge of the future and proved that Jesus was truly the promised Savior.

 # ACTIVITY

Write down a few predictions about what you think might happen tomorrow. Then, at the end of tomorrow, check to see if they came true. This "Prediction Check" helps you understand how amazing it is that God's prophecies always come true.

PRAYER

All-knowing God, thank You for revealing Your plans through the prophets. Thank You for sending Jesus, who fulfilled all the prophecies. Amen.

Chapter 223: The Angel Visits Mary

"The angel answered, 'The Holy Spirit will come on you, and the power of the Most High will overshadow you. So the holy one to be born will be called the Son of God.'" - Luke 1:35

In a town called Nazareth, there lived a young woman named Mary. She was engaged to a man named Joseph. One day, an angel named Gabriel appeared to Mary. The angel told her that she would have a baby, and this baby would be God's Son, Jesus. He would be great and would reign forever. Mary was surprised but humbly said, "I am the Lord's servant. May your word to me be fulfilled." This was a miraculous announcement, showing God's power to do the impossible.

 **ACTIVITY**

Imagine an angel suddenly appearing to you with an amazing message. How would you react? Draw a simple outline of an angel and a star, representing a heavenly message.

PRAYER

Miraculous God, thank You for the amazing story of Jesus' birth. Help me to be humble and willing to serve You, just like Mary. Amen.

Chapter 224: Mary's Song of Praise

"My soul glorifies the Lord and my spirit rejoices in God my Savior, for he has been mindful of the humble state of his servant. From now on all generations will call me blessed, for the Mighty One has done great things for me—holy is his name." - Luke 1:46-49

After the angel's visit, Mary went to visit her relative Elizabeth, who was also expecting a baby (John the Baptist). When Mary greeted Elizabeth, Elizabeth's baby leaped for joy, and Elizabeth was filled with the Holy Spirit. Mary then sang a beautiful song of praise to God.

She praised God for His greatness, His mercy, and His faithfulness to His promises. Mary's song shows her joyful heart and her deep trust in God.

 **ACTIVITY**

Think about something wonderful God has done for you. Write a short "Song of Praise" or a "Thank You" poem to God, expressing your joy and gratitude.

PRAYER

Praising God, thank You for Your greatness and Your mercy. Help me to always praise You with a joyful heart for all the wonderful things You do. Amen.

Chapter 225: The Angel Visits Joseph

"But after he had considered this, an angel of the Lord appeared to him in a dream and said, 'Joseph son of David, do not be afraid to take Mary home as your wife, because what is conceived in her is from the Holy Spirit. She will give birth to a son, and you are to give him the name Jesus, because he will save his people from their sins.'" - Matthew 1:20-21

Joseph, Mary's fiancé, was a righteous man. When he found out Mary was pregnant, he planned to quietly break off their engagement because he did not want to shame her.

An angel of the Lord appeared to Joseph in a dream and told him that the baby was from the Holy Spirit. The angel said Mary would give birth to a son, and Joseph was to name Him Jesus, because He would save His people from their sins. Joseph obeyed God's instruction and took Mary as his wife. This shows Joseph's obedience and his trust in God's plan.

 ## ACTIVITY

Think about a time you had a dream that helped you understand something important. Draw a simple thought bubble with a small angel inside, representing a dream message from God.

PRAYER

God, thank You for guiding Joseph through a dream. Help me to listen to Your guidance and to obey Your will, even when it is difficult to understand. Amen.

Chapter 226: Jesus Is Born

"While they were there, the time came for the baby to be born, and she gave birth to her firstborn, a son. She wrapped him in cloths and placed him in a manger, because there was no guest room available for them." - Luke 2:6-7

A decree went out from Caesar Augustus that everyone should go to their hometown to be registered. Joseph and Mary had to travel to Bethlehem, the town of David. While they were there, the time came for Mary to have her baby. There was no room for them in any inn, so they stayed in a stable. There, Mary gave birth to her firstborn son. She wrapped Him in cloths and placed Him in a manger, a feeding trough for animals. This was Jesus, the promised Savior, born in a humble place, just as the prophets had foretold.

 **ACTIVITY**

Imagine being born in a stable. What sounds and smells would there be? Draw a simple manger with a baby inside, surrounded by a few animals.

PRAYER

Dear God, thank You for sending Jesus, born in a humble stable. Thank You for coming to earth to save us. Amen.

Chapter 227: Shepherds Visit Jesus

"But the angel said to them, 'Do not be afraid. I bring you good news that will cause great joy for all the people. Today in the town of David a Savior has been born to you; he is the Messiah, the Lord.'" - Luke 2:10-11

In the fields near Bethlehem, shepherds were watching their sheep at night. Suddenly, an angel of the Lord appeared to them, and the glory of the Lord shone around them. The shepherds were terrified! The angel told them not to be afraid. He brought them good news of great joy: a Savior, who is the Messiah, the Lord, had been born in Bethlehem.

The angel told them they would find the baby wrapped in cloths and lying in a manger. Then, a huge group of angels appeared, praising God! The shepherds quickly went to Bethlehem and found Mary, Joseph, and the baby Jesus, just as the angel had said.

✎ ACTIVITY

Imagine you are a shepherd hearing the angels' announcement. What would you do first? Draw a simple star with lines radiating out, representing the glory of the Lord shining around the shepherds.

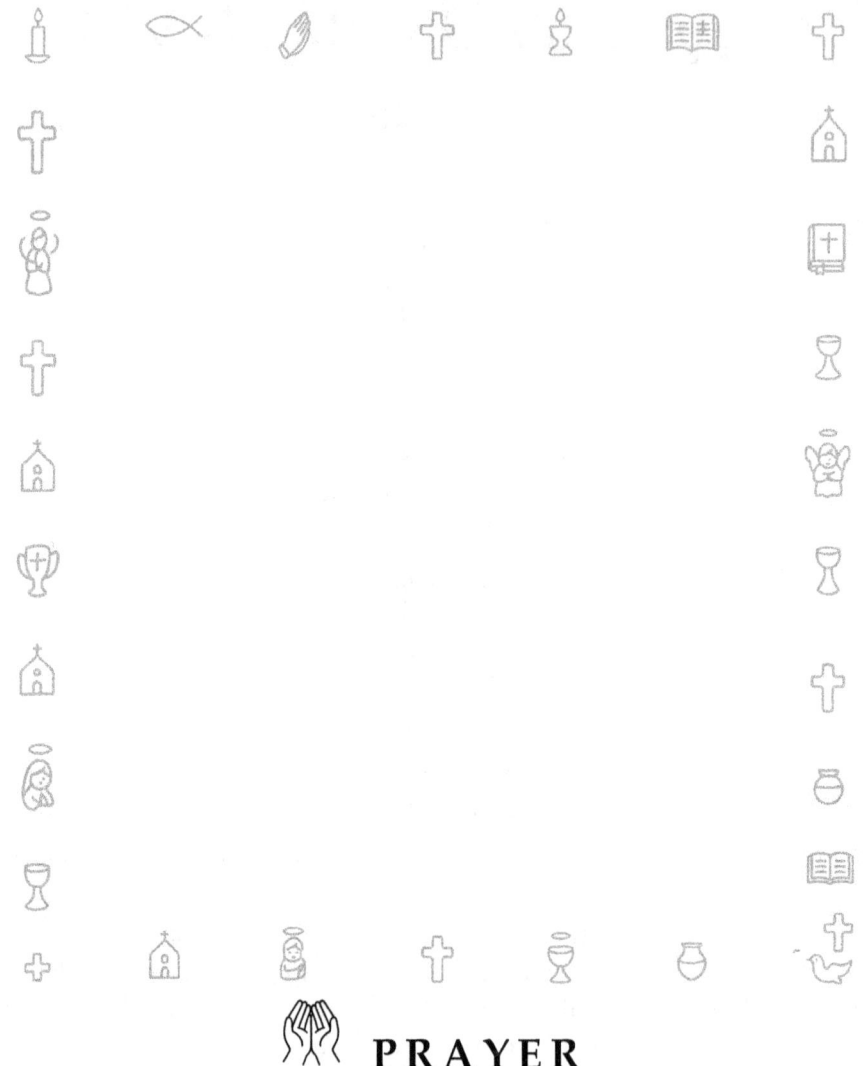

🙏 PRAYER

Joyful God, thank You for the good news of Jesus' birth. Thank You for inviting the shepherds to see Him. Help me to share this good news with others. Amen.

Chapter 228: Angels Announce Good News

"Suddenly a great company of the heavenly host appeared with the angel, praising God and saying, 'Glory to God in the highest heaven, and on earth peace to those on whom his favor rests.'" - Luke 2:13-14

The shepherds were not the only ones who received a special message about Jesus' birth. A whole army of angels appeared with the first angel, praising God and saying, "Glory to God in the highest heaven, and on earth peace to those on whom his favor rests."

This amazing sight and sound showed the incredible importance of Jesus' arrival. The angels were celebrating because God's plan to bring peace and salvation to the world was beginning. Their announcement was truly good news for everyone.

 **ACTIVITY**

Imagine you are part of that angel choir. What would it feel like to sing praises to God about Jesus' birth? Draw a picture of an angel singing, with musical notes floating around.

PRAYER

Heavenly Father, thank You for sending Your angels to announce the good news of Jesus' birth. Help me to give You glory and to share Your peace with others. Amen.

Chapter 229: Wise Men Follow the Star

"We saw his star when it rose and have come to worship him." - Matthew 2:2

After Jesus was born, a new star lit up the sky. Faraway scholars called Magi noticed it and knew God was announcing a special King. They packed gifts, loaded camels, and started the long journey to Bethlehem. The star guided them step-by-step until it stopped over the very place where Jesus was. When they finally saw Him, they were filled with joy, because real wisdom always leads us to worship Jesus.

 **ACTIVITY**

Go outside after dark and look for the brightest light you can find (maybe a streetlamp or the moon). Imagine following that light a long, long way just to meet Jesus!

 **PRAYER**

Dear God, thank You for leading the wise men and for leading me today. Help my heart point to Jesus like the star did. Amen.

Chapter 230: Gifts for the King

"Then they opened their treasures and presented him with gifts of gold, frankincense and myrrh." - Matthew 2:11

The Magi knelt before Jesus and gave Him precious gifts. Gold showed He is King. Frankincense, burned in worship, showed He is God. Myrrh, used for burials, hinted that Jesus would one day die for us. No gift could ever repay God's love, yet the wise men gladly offered their best. We can, too, by giving Jesus our time, talents, and hearts.

Like the Magi, our gifts can be thoughtful and costly: setting aside time to worship, using our abilities to serve others, and sharing what we have with those in need. When we give with joy, we're saying, "Jesus, You are worth my best," and our everyday choices, kind words, honest actions, generous hands, become a fragrant offering of love to our King.

 # ACTIVITY

Draw three gift boxes. Inside each, write or sketch one thing you can give Jesus this week (for example: time in prayer, sharing a toy, helping a friend).

PRAYER

King Jesus, everything I have belongs to You. Please take my small gifts and use them for Your glory. Amen.

Chapter 231: Escape to Egypt

"Get up...take the child and his mother and escape to Egypt." -
Matthew 2:13

An angel warned Joseph that King Herod wanted to hurt Jesus. That
very night Joseph, Mary, and little Jesus hurried off to Egypt. God
protected His Son by moving the family to safety until the danger passed.
Sometimes God answers our prayers by guiding us to a new place or
plan. Wherever He leads, He goes with us.

When life changes suddenly, new school, new town, new routines, we
can remember this story. God knows how to protect and guide our
families, too. If He says "go," we can obey quickly; if He says "wait," we
can trust His timing. He is our safe place, leading each step and watching
over us along the way.

 **ACTIVITY**

On a map (paper or digital), trace a pretend route from Bethlehem to Egypt. Talk about a time your family took a trip and God kept you safe.

PRAYER

Father, thank You for guiding Joseph and protecting Jesus. Help me listen when You nudge me to move or stay. Amen.

Chapter 232: Back to Nazareth

"He went and lived in a town called Nazareth." - Matthew 2:23

After Herod died, the angel told Joseph it was safe to return. The family settled in Nazareth, a small town where Jesus would grow up. It didn't look fancy, but it was exactly where God wanted Him. God often works in ordinary places and everyday routines to shape our hearts.

In Nazareth, Jesus learned, helped His family, and obeyed in small, daily ways. That reminds us God can use our homes, schools, and neighborhoods to grow us too. We don't need a big stage for God to do big work: faithfulness in little things is where His quiet miracles often begin.

 ## ACTIVITY

List three ordinary things in your day (like brushing teeth, packing lunch, walking the dog). Beside each, write one way you can honor God while doing it.

PRAYER

Lord, thank You for my normal days. Help me see that every place can be special when You are there. Amen.

Chapter 233: Jesus As A Boy

"The child grew and became strong; he was filled with wisdom, and the grace of God was on him." - Luke 2:40

Jesus learned to walk, talk, read Scripture, and help Joseph in the carpenter shop. He grew stronger and wiser, showing that growth takes time. God cares about our bodies, minds, and hearts. As we eat healthy food, study, play, and pray, we grow the way Jesus did, balanced and full of God's grace.

You can grow like Jesus by practicing small, steady habits: be kind even when it's hard, finish your work with care, move your body, and talk with God each day. Ask Him to help you learn new skills and make good choices, and celebrate the progress He's shaping in you

ACTIVITY

Measure your height on a doorway or wall chart. Under the mark write today's date and "Growing like Jesus!"

PRAYER

God, thank You for helping me grow inside and out. Please fill me with wisdom and grace each day. Amen.

Chapter 234: Jesus in the Temple

"After three days they found him in the temple courts, sitting among the teachers, listening to them and asking them questions."
- Luke 2:46

When Jesus was twelve, His family visited Jerusalem. On the journey home, Mary and Joseph realized Jesus wasn't with the group. They hurried back and found Him in the Temple, eagerly learning and sharing God's Word. Even at a young age Jesus loved being in His Father's house. Loving God means wanting to learn more about Him.

Afterward, Jesus went home to Nazareth with His parents and obeyed them, continuing to grow in wisdom and in favor with God and people. That shows us how to love God in everyday life: listen to your parents and teachers, ask good questions about the Bible, and make time to worship and pray.

 **ACTIVITY**

Write down one question you have about God or the Bible. Ask a parent, pastor, or teacher this week, just like Jesus asked questions!

PRAYER

Father, give me a curious heart that loves Your Word. Thank You for teachers who help me understand. Amen.

Chapter 235: Growing in Wisdom and Favor

"Jesus grew in wisdom and stature, and in favor with God and man." - Luke 2:52

Jesus didn't just get taller, He grew socially and spiritually, too. People enjoyed being around Him because His character reflected God's love. We grow in favor when we treat others kindly, obey parents, and spend time with God. Little choices each day add up to big growth over time.

Try simple, steady habits: greet others with kindness, listen before you speak, finish your work with care, and talk to God each day about your choices. Those small steps, repeated often, shape a strong heart that reflects God's love wherever you go.

 **ACTIVITY**

Make a "Grow Chart." Draw four branches labeled: Body, Mind, Friends, God. Write one goal on each branch (e.g., do ten jumping jacks, memorize a verse, say hello to a new classmate, pray before bed).

PRAYER

Lord, help me grow like Jesus, in wisdom, strength, friendships, and closeness with You. Amen.

Chapter 236: John the Baptist Prepares the Way

"Prepare the way for the Lord, make straight paths for him." - Matthew 3:3

Before Jesus began teaching, God sent John the Baptist to get people ready. John preached, "Turn away from wrong and turn toward God!" His job was like clearing rocks off a path so the King could arrive. When we admit our sins and open our hearts, we clear space for Jesus to work in us.

You can "clear the path" in your own life by telling God the truth about your choices, saying you're sorry, and asking Him to help you do what's right. Then show the change: be kind, tell the truth, and share with others. A heart that's ready for Jesus makes a straight road for His love to shine through you.

 ACTIVITY

Sweep a small area (porch, driveway, bedroom floor). As you clean, pray that God will sweep away anything in your heart that blocks you from Him.

 PRAYER

Holy God, please clear my heart of selfishness and make it ready for Jesus every day. Amen.

Chapter 237: Jesus Is Baptized

"As soon as Jesus was baptized...heaven was opened." - Matthew 3:16

Although Jesus had no sin, He chose to be baptized by John to show His obedience and to set an example for us. When He came up from the water, heaven opened, the Spirit descended like a dove, and God the Father said, "This is my Son, whom I love." All three Persons of the Trinity celebrated together!

Baptism shows on the outside what's happening on the inside: a heart choosing to follow God. Jesus' baptism reminds us to listen to the Father, welcome the Spirit's leading, and live in a way that brings joy to God.

 ## ACTIVITY

Look up a picture or video of a dove. Think about how softly it lands. That's a picture of the Holy Spirit resting on Jesus, and on us when we follow Him.

 ## PRAYER

Father, thank You for showing Your love for Jesus at His baptism. Help me obey You and follow Jesus' example. Amen.

Chapter 238: The Holy Spirit Descends

"and the Holy Spirit descended on him in bodily form like a dove. And a voice came from heaven: "You are my Son, whom I love; with you I am well pleased." - Luke 3:22

The Holy Spirit empowered Jesus for His ministry. The Spirit is God living in us, giving courage, wisdom, and love to do what's right. Just as the Spirit rested on Jesus, He dwells in every believer today, guiding us one step at a time.

You can welcome His help each day by praying, "Holy Spirit, lead me." He gives gentle nudges to choose kindness, truth, and self-control, and He grows good fruit in our lives like love, joy, and peace. When you're unsure what to do, pause, listen, and follow His quiet guidance.

 ## ACTIVITY

Close your eyes and take three slow breaths. As you breathe, whisper, "Holy Spirit, guide me." Notice the calm He brings.

 ## PRAYER

Holy Spirit, thank You for living in me. Lead my thoughts, words, and actions today. Amen.

Chapter 239: Jesus Is Tempted

"Jesus was led by the Spirit into the wilderness to be tempted by the devil." - Matthew 4:1

Right after His baptism, Jesus faced tough temptations in the desert. He was hungry, lonely, and tired, yet He answered every temptation with Scripture: "It is written...." Jesus showed us that God's Word is our best defense against wrong choices. Because Jesus won over temptation, He can help us overcome, too.

 ACTIVITY

Choose one short Bible verse about courage or obedience. Write it on a card and keep it in your pocket for quick "desert-time" help.

 **PRAYER**

Jesus, thank You for beating temptation. Help me remember Your Word when I'm tempted and give me strength to choose what's right. Amen.

Chapter 240: Jesus Begins His Ministry

"From that time on Jesus began to preach, 'Repent, for the kingdom of heaven has come near.'" - Matthew 4:17

After defeating temptation, Jesus traveled through Galilee announcing good news: God's kingdom, His loving rule, is here! Jesus healed the sick, comforted the hurting, and invited everyone to follow Him. His ministry shows God's heart: rescuing people and restoring broken lives. We get to be part of His mission, sharing His love wherever we go.

 **ACTIVITY**

Draw a crown and inside it write one way you can show someone God's kingdom today (like encouraging a classmate or sharing a snack).

PRAYER

King Jesus, thank You for bringing God's kingdom close. Use me to spread Your love and kindness today. Amen.

Chapter 241: Jesus Calls His First Disciples

"As Jesus was walking beside the Sea of Galilee, he saw two brothers, Simon called Peter and his brother Andrew. They were casting a net into the lake, for they were fishermen. 'Come, follow me,' Jesus said, 'and I will send you out to fish for people.'" - Matthew 4:18-19

After beginning His ministry, Jesus walked by the Sea of Galilee and saw two brothers, Simon (who would later be called Peter) and Andrew, casting a net into the lake. Jesus called out to them, "Come, follow me, and I will send you out to fish for people." Immediately, they left their nets and followed Him. Then He saw two more brothers, James and John, also fishermen, and called them. They left their boat and their father and followed Jesus. This shows that following Jesus means being ready to leave things behind and obey His call.

 **ACTIVITY**

Imagine you are a fisherman, and Jesus calls you. What would you do? Draw a simple fishing net. Inside the net, draw small stick figures representing "people" you could tell about Jesus.

PRAYER

Calling Jesus, thank You for inviting people to follow You. Help me to be ready to follow You wherever You lead and to share Your good news with others. Amen.

Chapter 242: The Wedding at Cana

"Jesus said to the servants, "Fill the jars with water"; so they filled them to the brim. Then he told them, "Now draw some out and take it to the master of the banquet." They did so, and the master of the banquet tasted the water that had been turned into wine. He did not realize where it had come from, though the servants who had drawn the water knew. Then he called the bridegroom aside" - John 2:7-9

Jesus, His mother Mary, and His disciples were invited to a wedding in Cana. During the celebration, the wine ran out, which would have been very embarrassing for the hosts. Mary told Jesus about the problem. Jesus told the servants to fill six large stone jars with water. Then, He told them to draw some out and take it to the master of the banquet. The master tasted it and discovered it was the best wine!

This was Jesus' first miracle, showing His power over creation and revealing His glory to His disciples.

 ## ACTIVITY

Find two clear glasses. Fill one with water. In the other, put a few drops of food coloring and mix it in. This "Color Change" reminds you of how Jesus changed water into wine, showing His power.

 ## PRAYER

Miraculous Jesus, thank You for showing Your power and glory. Help me to trust You with my problems, knowing You can do amazing things. Amen.

Chapter 243: Jesus Cleanses the Temple

"In the temple courts he found people selling cattle, sheep and doves, and others sitting at tables exchanging money. So he made a whip out of cords, and drove all from the temple courts, both sheep and cattle; he scattered the coins of the money changers and overturned their tables." - John 2:14-15

Jesus went to Jerusalem for the Passover. When He entered the Temple courts, He saw people selling animals for sacrifices and exchanging money. These activities were important, but they were being done in a disrespectful way, turning God's house of prayer into a marketplace. Jesus was angry because they were dishonoring God's holy place. He overturned tables and drove out the animals and sellers. Jesus showed His passion for God's holiness and His desire for true worship.

 **ACTIVITY**

Think about a place that is special or holy to you (like a church, your quiet prayer spot, or a special family area). What makes it special? Draw a simple church building with a cross on top, representing a house of prayer.

PRAYER

Holy Jesus, thank You for showing us the importance of honoring God. Help me to treat all holy things with respect and to worship God with a pure heart. Amen.

Chapter 244: Nicodemus Visits Jesus

"For God so loved the world that he gave his one and only Son, that whoever believes in him shall not perish but have eternal life." - John 3:16

Nicodemus was a Pharisee, a religious leader, who came to Jesus secretly at night. He knew Jesus was a teacher sent from God because of the miracles He performed. Jesus told Nicodemus that no one can see the kingdom of God unless they are "born again." This means having a spiritual rebirth, a new life from God, through faith in Jesus. Nicodemus was confused at first, but Jesus explained that God loved the world so much that He sent His Son so that whoever believes in Him can have eternal life.

ACTIVITY

Imagine you are planting a seed. What does it need to grow into a new plant? Draw a tiny seed turning into a small sprout, representing being "born again" into new life with Jesus.

PRAYER

Loving God, thank You for loving the world so much that You sent Jesus. Help me to believe in Him and to experience the new life You offer. Amen.

Chapter 245: Jesus and the Samaritan Woman

"Jesus answered, 'Everyone who drinks this water will be thirsty again, but whoever drinks the water I give them will never thirst. Indeed, the water I give them will become in them a spring of water welling up to eternal life.'" - John 4:13-14

Jesus traveled through Samaria, a place Jews usually avoided. He stopped at a well and asked a Samaritan woman for a drink. This was unusual because Jews and Samaritans did not usually interact. Jesus told her about "living water" that would quench her spiritual thirst forever. He knew all about her life, even her secret sins. The woman realized Jesus was the Messiah and went to tell everyone in her town. Many Samaritans believed in Jesus because of her testimony. This shows that Jesus loves everyone, no matter their background, and offers them new life.

 **ACTIVITY**

Get a glass of water and drink it slowly, thinking about how it refreshes your body. Then, think about how Jesus offers "living water" to refresh your spirit. Draw a simple cup overflowing with water.

PRAYER

Jesus, thank You for offering living water that satisfies my soul. Help me to share Your good news with everyone, just like the Samaritan woman did. Amen.

Chapter 246: Jesus Heals the Official's Son

"So he asked Jesus to come down and heal his son, who was about to die. 'Go,' Jesus replied, 'your son will live.' The man took Jesus at his word and departed." - John 4:47-50

A royal official in Capernaum had a son who was very sick and dying. He heard that Jesus was in Cana and desperately went to Him, begging Jesus to come and heal his son. Jesus told the official, "Go; your son will live." The official believed Jesus' word and started on his way home. Before he even reached his house, his servants met him with the good news that his son was alive and well! Jesus healed the boy from a distance, showing His power is not limited by space. This miracle led the official and his whole household to believe.

 **ACTIVITY**

Imagine you have a special message you need to send to someone far away. How would you send it? Draw a simple phone or a letter with a heart on it, symbolizing how Jesus' word can travel and heal from a distance.

PRAYER

Healing Jesus, thank You for Your power to heal, even from far away. Help me to believe Your word and to trust You with the things I cannot see. Amen.

Chapter 247: Jesus Teaches in Nazareth

"He began by saying to them, 'Today this scripture is fulfilled in your hearing.'" - Luke 4:21

Jesus returned to Nazareth, the town where He grew up. On the Sabbath, He went into the synagogue and stood up to read. He read from the prophet Isaiah, a passage that spoke about the Messiah bringing good news to the poor, freedom to prisoners, sight to the blind, and setting the oppressed free. Jesus then declared, "Today this scripture is fulfilled in your hearing." At first, people were amazed, but then they remembered He was just "Joseph's son" and rejected Him. This shows that even in His hometown, some people struggled to believe in Jesus because they thought they knew Him too well.

 ACTIVITY

Think about a time you tried to share something exciting, but someone did not believe you. How did that feel? Write down one thing you believe about Jesus. Draw a simple open book, representing the Scripture Jesus read.

PRAYER

Jesus, thank You for bringing good news and freedom. Help me to truly see You for who You are, not just what I expect, and to believe in You. Amen.

Chapter 248: Peter Catches Many Fish

"When he had finished speaking, he said to Simon, 'Put out into deep water, and let down the nets for a catch.' Simon answered, 'Master, we've worked hard all night and haven't caught anything. But because you say so, I will let down the nets.' When they had done so, they caught such a large number of fish that their nets began to break." - Luke 5:4-6

One day, Jesus was teaching by the Lake of Gennesaret, and a crowd was pressing in on Him. He saw two boats, and He got into Simon Peter's boat, asking him to push out a little from the shore. After teaching, Jesus told Peter to go out into deep water and let down his nets for a catch.

Peter had been fishing all night and caught nothing, but he obeyed Jesus. When they pulled in the nets, they caught such a huge number of fish that their nets began to break, and they had to call for help from another boat! This miracle showed Jesus' power to provide abundantly and His authority over creation. It also showed Peter that Jesus was truly special.

ACTIVITY

Get a small container (like a bowl) and some small objects (like beads or paper clips) to represent fish. Try to scoop them out with a small spoon. Then, imagine a huge scoop that catches them all! This "Abundant Catch" activity helps visualize the miracle.

PRAYER

Providing Jesus, thank You for Your amazing power to provide. Help me to obey You, even when I am tired or doubtful, and to trust You for abundant blessings. Amen.

Chapter 249: Jesus Heals a Leper

"A man with leprosy came to him and begged him on his knees, 'If you are willing, you can make me clean.' Jesus was indignant. He reached out his hand and touched the man. 'I am willing,' he said. 'Be clean!' Immediately the leprosy left him." - Mark 1:40-42

In Jesus' time, people with leprosy had a terrible skin disease and were forced to live apart from everyone else. They were considered "unclean." One day, a man with leprosy came to Jesus, knelt before Him, and said, "Lord, if you are willing, you can make me clean." Jesus, full of compassion, reached out His hand and touched the man, which no one else would dare to do. He said, "I am willing. Be clean!" Immediately, the leprosy left him. Jesus showed His compassion for outcasts and His power to heal and make clean.

 **ACTIVITY**

Think about someone who might feel left out or "unclean" (maybe someone new, or someone who is different). What is one way you can reach out to them and show kindness, just as Jesus reached out to the leper? Draw two hands reaching out to connect.

PRAYER

Compassionate Jesus, thank You for loving those who are left out. Help me to show kindness and compassion to everyone, just as You do. Amen.

Chapter 250: Jesus Heals a Paralyzed Man

"When Jesus saw their faith, he said to the paralyzed man, 'Son, your sins are forgiven.' ... He said to the man, 'I tell you, get up, take your mat and go home.' He got up, took his mat and walked out in full view of them all." - Mark 2:5, 11-12

Jesus was teaching in a house, and it was so crowded that there was no room left, not even at the door. Four men brought their paralyzed friend on a mat, but they could not get him inside. So, they climbed onto the roof, made an opening, and lowered their friend right down in front of Jesus! Jesus saw their great faith. He said to the paralyzed man, "Son, your sins are forgiven."

Then, to show He had the authority to forgive sins, Jesus told the man to pick up his mat and walk. Immediately, the man stood up, picked up his mat, and walked out, praising God! This miracle showed Jesus' power over sickness and His unique authority to forgive sins.

 ## ACTIVITY

Find a small mat or towel. Place a toy on it. Imagine trying to get the toy into a crowded room. Then, imagine lowering it from the ceiling! This "Creative Delivery" helps you think about the friends' determination.

 ## PRAYER

Forgiving Jesus, thank You for Your power to heal and to forgive sins. Help me to have faith like the paralyzed man's friends and to bring others to You. Amen.

Chapter 251: Jesus Calls Matthew

"As Jesus went on from there, he saw a man named Matthew sitting at the tax collector's booth. 'Follow me,' he told him, and Matthew got up and followed him." - Matthew 9:9

Jesus was walking by the Sea of Galilee and saw a tax collector named Matthew sitting at his tax collector's booth. Tax collectors were often disliked because they worked for the Roman government and sometimes cheated people. But Jesus called out to Matthew, "Follow me."

And just like the fishermen, Matthew immediately got up, left everything behind, and followed Jesus. Later, Matthew even hosted a dinner for Jesus at his house, and many other tax collectors and "sinners" came to eat with them. This shows that Jesus calls all kinds of people, even those society looks down on, and He came to save sinners.

 **ACTIVITY**

Imagine you have a job you do every day. What would it be like to suddenly leave it all to follow someone new? Draw a simple table with some coins on it, and then draw a path leading away from it, symbolizing Matthew leaving his old life to follow Jesus.

PRAYER

Calling Jesus, thank You for calling all kinds of people to follow You. Help me to be ready to leave anything behind that keeps me from You and to follow You completely. Amen.

Chapter 252: Jesus Heals on the Sabbath

"Then Jesus asked them, 'Which is lawful on the Sabbath: to do good or to do evil, to save life or to destroy it?' But they remained silent. He looked around at them in anger and, deeply distressed at their stubborn hearts, said to the man, 'Stretch out your hand.' He stretched it out, and his hand was completely restored." - Mark 3:4-5

The Sabbath was a special day of rest for the Jewish people, set apart to honor God. Religious leaders, the Pharisees, had many strict rules about what could and could not be done on the Sabbath. One Sabbath, Jesus went into a synagogue and saw a man with a shriveled hand.

The Pharisees watched to see if Jesus would heal on the Sabbath so they could accuse Him. Jesus knew their thoughts. He asked, "Which is lawful on the Sabbath: to do good or to do evil, to save life or to destroy it?" Then He told the man to stretch out his hand, and it was completely restored! Jesus showed that it is always right to do good and to help people, even on the Sabbath.

 ## ACTIVITY

Think about a time you saw someone needing help. What did you do? Draw a hand that looks a little withered, and next to it, draw a hand that is strong and healthy, symbolizing healing.

PRAYER

Healing Jesus, thank You for always doing good and for caring about people more than rules. Help me to always choose to do good and to help others, just like You. Amen.

Chapter 253: Choosing the Twelve Disciples

"One of those days Jesus went out to a mountainside to pray, and spent the night praying to God. When morning came, he called his disciples to him and chose twelve of them, whom he also designated apostles." - Luke 6:12-13

Jesus had many followers, but He chose twelve special men to be His closest disciples, or apostles. He spent a whole night praying to God before He made this important choice. These twelve men would learn from Jesus, witness His miracles, and eventually be sent out to preach and heal. They came from different backgrounds, but Jesus chose them all. This shows that Jesus carefully chooses those He wants to work closely with, and He prepares them for important tasks.

 **ACTIVITY**

Imagine you are picking a team for a very important project. What qualities would you look for? Draw twelve small circles in a group, with one larger circle in the middle, representing Jesus and His twelve disciples.

PRAYER

Jesus, thank You for choosing Your disciples and for choosing me to be Your follower. Help me to learn from You and to be ready to serve You. Amen.

Chapter 254: The Sermon on the Mount Begins

"Now when Jesus saw the crowds, he went up on a mountainside and sat down. His disciples came to him, and he began to teach them." - Matthew 5:1-2

After choosing His twelve disciples, Jesus went up on a mountainside and began to teach a large crowd of people. This famous teaching is called the Sermon on the Mount. In it, Jesus taught about what it means to live in God's kingdom. He taught about true happiness, how to live righteously, and how to relate to God and others. This sermon gives us many important lessons about how to live a life that pleases God.

 ## ACTIVITY

Find a quiet spot, perhaps outside or in a cozy corner. Imagine Jesus sitting there, ready to teach you. Write down one question you would ask Jesus if you could.

PRAYER

Teaching Jesus, thank You for Your wise words in the Sermon on the Mount. Open my heart and mind to learn from Your teachings and to live according to Your kingdom. Amen.

Chapter 255: The Beatitudes

"Blessed are the poor in spirit, for theirs is the kingdom of heaven." - *Matthew 5:3*

The Sermon on the Mount begins with a section called the Beatitudes. "Blessed are..." means "Happy are..." or "Fortunate are..." Jesus taught that true happiness comes from having certain qualities in our hearts, like being poor in spirit (knowing we need God), mourning (being sad about sin), being gentle, hungering for righteousness, being merciful, pure in heart, peacemakers, and being persecuted for doing right.

These are not easy qualities, but Jesus promises great blessings to those who live this way.

ACTIVITY

Choose one of the Beatitudes (e.g., "Blessed are the peacemakers"). Think about how you can practice that quality today. Draw a simple happy face with a halo, representing true blessedness.

PRAYER

Jesus, thank You for teaching me what true happiness means. Help me to develop the qualities of Your kingdom so I can be truly blessed. Amen.

Chapter 256: Salt and Light

"You are the salt of the earth. But if the salt loses its saltiness, how can it be made salty again? ... You are the light of the world. A town built on a hill cannot be hidden." - Matthew 5:13-14

In the Sermon on the Mount, Jesus told His followers, "You are the salt of the earth" and "You are the light of the world." Salt makes food taste better and preserves it. Light helps us see and guides us. Jesus means that His followers should make the world a better place by living lives that honor God. We should spread God's goodness and truth, helping others see Him and guiding them to Him. We are meant to make a difference!

 **ACTIVITY**

Find a pinch of salt and taste it. Then, turn on a flashlight in a dim room. Think about how these simple things make a big difference. Draw a salt shaker and a lightbulb next to each other.

PRAYER

Jesus, thank You for calling me to be salt and light in the world. Help me to make a positive difference for You wherever I go. Amen.

Chapter 257: Jesus Fulfills the Law

"Do not think that I have come to abolish the Law or the Prophets; I have not come to abolish them but to fulfill them." - Matthew 5:17

Some people thought Jesus had come to get rid of God's Old Testament laws. But Jesus said, "Do not think that I have come to abolish the Law or the Prophets; I have not come to abolish them but to fulfill them." Jesus perfectly obeyed all of God's laws. He lived the perfect life that no one else could.

He also fulfilled the prophecies and the meaning of the laws, showing that they all pointed to Him. Because Jesus fulfilled the law, we can have a right relationship with God through Him.

 **ACTIVITY**

Think about a puzzle with many pieces. How does each piece fit together to make the complete picture? Draw a simple puzzle with a few pieces missing, and then draw Jesus as the final piece that completes it.

PRAYER

Jesus, thank You for perfectly fulfilling God's law. Help me to understand how all of Scripture points to You and Your perfect life. Amen.

Chapter 258: Loving Our Enemies

"You have heard that it was said, 'Love your neighbor and hate your enemy.' But I tell you, love your enemies and pray for those who persecute you." - Matthew 5:43-44

In the Sermon on the Mount, Jesus taught something very challenging: "Love your enemies and pray for those who persecute you." This is not an easy command! It means choosing to show kindness and good will even to people who are mean to us or who do not like us. It is easy to love our friends, but loving our enemies shows a special kind of love, God's love, working through us.

 ## ACTIVITY

Think about someone who is difficult to get along with. Write their name on a small piece of paper. Pray for them, asking God to help you love them and for God to bless them. This is your "Enemy Prayer."

 ## PRAYER

Loving Jesus, it is hard to love my enemies. Please fill my heart with Your love and help me to pray for and be kind to those who are difficult. Amen.

Chapter 259: Giving to the Needy

"So when you give to the needy, do not announce it with trumpets, as the hypocrites do in the synagogues and on the streets, to be honored by others. Truly I tell you, they have received their reward in full. But when you give to the needy, do not let your left hand know what your right hand is doing, so that your giving may be in secret. Then your Father, who sees what is done in secret, will reward you." - Matthew 6:2-4

Jesus taught about giving to the needy. He said that when we give to others, we should not do it to show off or to get praise from people. We should give quietly and sincerely, because God sees what we do in secret. Our giving should come from a heart that wants to help others and honor God. God loves a cheerful giver.

 **ACTIVITY**

Find a small coin or dollar bill. Think about how you could secretly give it to help someone in need (e.g., put it in a charity box, give it to a parent for a good cause). Draw a simple hand dropping a coin into a box.

PRAYER

Generous God, thank You for teaching me to give. Help me to give cheerfully and secretly, wanting only to honor You and help others. Amen.

Chapter 260: How to Pray

"This, then, is how you should pray: 'Our Father in heaven, hallowed be your name, your kingdom come, your will be done, on earth as it is in heaven.'" - Matthew 6:9-10

The disciples asked Jesus how to pray, and Jesus gave them a model prayer, often called the Lord's Prayer. He taught them to start by honoring God's name, then to pray for God's kingdom to come and His will to be done. He also taught them to pray for their daily needs, for forgiveness, and for protection from temptation. This prayer teaches us how to talk to God with respect, trust, and a focus on His kingdom.

📝 ACTIVITY

Write down the first few lines of the Lord's Prayer. Practice saying them slowly, thinking about what each part means. Draw a simple pair of hands folded in prayer.

🙏 PRAYER

Dear God, thank You for teaching me how to pray. Help me to talk with You honestly and to pray for Your will to be done in my life and in the world. Amen.

Chapter 261: The Lord's Prayer

"Give us today our daily bread. And forgive us our debts, as we also have forgiven our debtors. And lead us not into temptation, but deliver us from the evil one." - Matthew 6:11-13

Jesus continued teaching His disciples the Lord's Prayer. After praying for God's name and kingdom, He taught them to pray for their daily bread, for forgiveness of their sins (just as they forgive others), and for deliverance from evil. This prayer covers all the important things: honoring God, trusting Him for our needs, seeking His forgiveness, forgiving others, and asking for His protection. It is a perfect example of how to pray simply and sincerely.

 **ACTIVITY**

Write down one thing you are thankful for today (your "daily bread"). Then, think of one person you need to forgive. This "Daily Prayer Check-in" helps you practice parts of the Lord's Prayer.

PRAYER

Our Father, thank You for teaching me to pray. Help me to trust You for my daily needs, to forgive others, and to seek Your protection. Amen.

Chapter 262: Storing Up Treasures in Heaven

"Do not store up for yourselves treasures on earth, where moths and vermin destroy, and where thieves break in and steal. But store up for yourselves treasures in heaven, where moths and vermin do not destroy, and where thieves do not break in and steal. For where your treasure is, there your heart will be also." - Matthew 6:19-21

Jesus taught that we should not store up treasures on earth, where they can be stolen or ruined. Instead, we should store up treasures in heaven, where they are safe forever. Heavenly treasures are not money or possessions; they are things like acts of kindness, serving God, and loving others. When we focus on eternal things, our hearts will be in the right place, centered on God.

ACTIVITY

Draw two treasure chests. Label one "Earthly Treasures" and the other "Heavenly Treasures." Draw or write things in each (e.g., toys in earthly, helping hands in heavenly). Think about which chest you want to fill.

PRAYER

God, thank You for teaching me about heavenly treasures. Help me to focus my heart on You and on eternal things, not just on things here on earth. Amen.

Chapter 263: Do Not Worry

"Therefore I tell you, do not worry about your life, what you will eat or drink; or about your body, what you will wear. Is not life more than food, and the body more than clothes? Look at the birds of the air; they do not sow or reap or store away in barns, and yet your heavenly Father feeds them. Are you not much more valuable than they?" - Matthew 6:25-26

Jesus taught His followers not to worry about what they would eat, drink, or wear. He pointed to the birds of the air, which God feeds, and the lilies of the field, which God clothes beautifully. If God cares for birds and flowers, how much more will He care for us, His children? Worrying does not add a single hour to our lives. Instead of worrying, Jesus told us to seek God's kingdom first, and He will provide everything we need.

 ## ACTIVITY

Find a picture of a bird or a flower. Look at its details and beauty. This "Nature's Trust" reminds you that God cares for even the smallest parts of His creation, and He cares for you even more.

 ## PRAYER

Caring God, thank You for reminding me not to worry. Help me to trust You completely with all my needs, knowing You will always provide for me. Amen.

Chapter 264: Judging Others

"Do not judge, or you too will be judged. For in the same way you judge others, you will be judged, and with the measure you use, it will be measured to you." - Matthew 7:1-2

Jesus taught, "Do not judge, or you too will be judged." This means we should not criticize or condemn others, especially when we have our own faults. Jesus used the example of a "plank in your own eye" while trying to remove a "speck" from someone else's eye. It is easy to see other people's mistakes, but harder to see our own. Instead of judging, we should focus on examining our own hearts and seeking to help others with love and humility.

 ACTIVITY

Look in a mirror. What do you see? Now, imagine trying to see a tiny speck in someone else's eye while you have something big in your own! This "Mirror Reflection" helps you think about judging.

 PRAYER

Humble Jesus, help me not to judge others. Help me to see my own heart clearly and to show love and grace to everyone I meet. Amen.

Chapter 265: Ask, Seek, Knock

"Ask and it will be given to you; seek and you will find; knock and the door will be opened to you. For everyone who asks receives; the one who seeks finds; and to the one who knocks, the door will be opened." - Matthew 7:7-8

Jesus encouraged His followers to ask, seek, and knock when they pray. He promised, "Ask and it will be given to you; seek and you will find; knock and the door will be opened to you." This means God wants us to be persistent and earnest in our prayers. Just as a good father gives good gifts to his children, our heavenly Father loves to give good gifts to those who ask Him.

 **ACTIVITY**

Play a simple "Hide and Seek" game with a small object. Hide it and have a family member find it. This "Seeking Game" reminds you of seeking God in prayer.

 **PRAYER**

Listening God, thank You for inviting me to ask, seek, and knock. Help me to be persistent in prayer and to trust that You love to give good gifts. Amen.

Chapter 266: The Narrow and Wide Gates

"Enter through the narrow gate. For wide is the gate and broad is the road that leads to destruction, and many enter through it. But small is the gate and narrow the road that leads to life, and only a few find it." - Matthew 7:13-14

Jesus taught about two paths: a wide gate and a narrow gate. The wide gate leads to destruction, and many people go through it. The narrow gate leads to life, and only a few find it. This means that following Jesus and living God's way is not always the easiest or most popular path. It requires effort and commitment. But the narrow path leads to true life and a relationship with God.

 **ACTIVITY**

Draw two paths. Make one very wide and easy, and the other narrow and a bit winding. At the end of the narrow path, draw a bright light or a happy face. This "Two Paths" drawing helps you visualize Jesus' teaching.

PRAYER

Guiding Jesus, thank You for showing me the path to life. Help me to choose the narrow gate and to follow You every day, even when it is difficult. Amen.

Chapter 267: Building on the Rock

"Therefore everyone who hears these words of mine and puts them into practice is like the wise man who built his house on the rock. The rain came down, the streams rose, and the winds blew and beat against that house; yet it did not fall, because it had its foundation on the rock." - Matthew 7:24-25

Jesus ended the Sermon on the Mount with a parable about two builders. One built his house on sand, and when the storms came, the house collapsed. The other built his house on solid rock, and when the storms came, the house stood firm. Jesus said that anyone who hears His words and puts them into practice is like the wise builder who built on the rock. Hearing Jesus' words is important, but obeying them is what makes our lives strong and stable, able to withstand life's challenges.

 **ACTIVITY**

Find a small toy house or build one with blocks. Try placing it on a soft pillow (sand) and then on a hard, flat surface (rock). Gently shake the surface. This "Stable Foundation" experiment shows the difference.

PRAYER

Strong Jesus, thank You for being my solid rock. Help me to not only hear Your words but to put them into practice, so my life can be built on a strong foundation. Amen.

Chapter 268: Jesus Heals a Centurion's Servant

"When Jesus heard this, he was amazed and said to those following him, 'Truly I tell you, I have not found anyone in Israel with such great faith. ... Then Jesus said to the centurion, 'Go! Let it be done just as you believed it would.' And the servant was healed at that moment." - Matthew 8:10, 13

A Roman centurion, a military officer, came to Jesus, begging Him to heal his servant who was paralyzed and suffering greatly. The centurion was a Gentile, not a Jew, but he had great faith. He told Jesus, "Lord, I do not deserve to have you come under my roof. But just say the word, and my servant will be healed."

Jesus was amazed by his faith and said He had not found such great faith in all of Israel. Immediately, the servant was healed. This shows

Jesus' power to heal and His delight in great faith, no matter who it comes from.

 # ACTIVITY

Think about a time you believed something would happen, and it did. How did that feel? Draw a simple word bubble with "Heal!" inside it, representing Jesus' powerful word.

PRAYER

Healing Jesus, thank You for Your power to heal and for valuing great faith. Help me to have strong faith in Your word and to trust You completely. Amen.

Chapter 269: Jesus Raises a Widow's Son

"When the Lord saw her, his heart went out to her and he said, 'Don't cry.' Then he went up and touched the bier they were carrying him on, and the bearers stood still. He said, 'Young man, I say to you, get up!' The dead man sat up and began to talk, and Jesus gave him back to his mother." - Luke 7:13-15

As Jesus approached a town called Nain, He saw a funeral procession. A young man had died, and he was the only son of a widow, which meant she had no one left to care for her. Jesus felt deep compassion for the grieving mother. He went up to the coffin, touched it, and commanded, "Young man, I say to you, get up!" Immediately, the dead man sat up and began to talk! Jesus gave him back to his mother. This miracle showed Jesus' power over death and His tender compassion for those who are hurting.

ACTIVITY

Think about a time you felt sad for someone. What did you do to show you cared? Draw a simple figure sitting up from a lying position, representing life being restored.

PRAYER

Compassionate Jesus, thank You for Your power over death and for Your tender heart towards those who grieve. Help me to show compassion to others who are sad. Amen.

Chapter 270: Jesus Calms the Storm

"He got up, rebuked the wind and the raging waters; the storm subsided, and all was calm. 'Where is your faith?' he asked his disciples." - Luke 8:24-25

One evening, Jesus and His disciples got into a boat to cross to the other side of the lake. Jesus fell asleep. Suddenly, a furious storm came up on the lake, with huge waves crashing over the boat, and it began to fill with water. The disciples were terrified and woke Jesus, crying, "Teacher, don't you care if we drown?"

Rising from His sleep, Jesus commanded the wind and waves to be still, and at once, perfect calm settled over the lake. This miracle showed Jesus' power over nature and challenged His disciples to trust Him even in the midst of fear.

 **ACTIVITY**

Take a deep breath and then let it out slowly. Imagine blowing away worries like clouds. Draw a stormy scene on one side of a paper and a calm, peaceful scene on the other, representing Jesus calming the storm.

PRAYER

Powerful Jesus, thank You for Your power over storms, both in nature and in my life. Help me to trust You and to have faith, even when I am afraid. Amen.

Chapter 271: Jesus Heals a Demon-Possessed Man

"When Jesus stepped ashore, he was met by a demon-possessed man from the town. For a long time this man had not worn clothes or lived in a house, but had lived in the tombs. When he saw Jesus, he cried out and fell at his feet, shouting at the top of his voice, 'What do you want with me, Jesus, Son of the Most High God?'" - Luke 8:27-28

After crossing the lake, Jesus and His disciples arrived in the region of the Gerasenes. A man who was possessed by many evil spirits lived among the tombs. He was so wild that no one could control him. When he saw Jesus, he cried out. Jesus commanded the evil spirits to come out of him.

The spirits begged Jesus to send them into a herd of pigs nearby, and Jesus allowed it. The pigs rushed down a steep bank into the lake and drowned. The man was completely healed and sitting calmly at Jesus' feet. This miracle showed Jesus' absolute authority over evil spirits.

 **ACTIVITY**

Think about a time you felt really out of control or overwhelmed by something. How did you find peace again? Draw a simple chain breaking, symbolizing freedom from something that holds you captive.

PRAYER

Powerful Jesus, thank You for Your authority over all evil. Help me to trust You when I feel overwhelmed and to find freedom and peace in Your presence. Amen.

Chapter 272: Jesus Heals a Woman and Raises a Girl

"Your faith has healed you. Go in peace." - Luke 8:48

Jesus performed two miracles in one day that showed how much He cares for people, no matter their age or situation. A woman who had been sick for 12 years believed that just touching Jesus' clothes would heal her, and it did! At the same time, a man named Jairus asked Jesus to help his daughter who was very sick. Even after the girl died, Jesus went to her house, took her by the hand, and brought her back to life. These miracles show us that Jesus hears our prayers, cares about our problems, and has the power to help in ways that no one else can. Faith connects us to His love and power.

 **ACTIVITY**

Draw two hearts, one for the woman and one for the girl. Inside each heart, write the word "FAITH."

PRAYER

Jesus, thank You for healing and loving people. Help me to trust You with all my heart. Amen.

Chapter 273: Jesus Feeds Five Thousand

"They all ate and were satisfied." - Matthew 14:20

When a huge crowd came to hear Jesus teach, they stayed so long that they became hungry. The disciples worried because there wasn't enough food to feed everyone. But one boy offered his small lunch of five loaves of bread and two fish. Jesus thanked God for the food, and then a miracle happened: the food multiplied until over 5,000 people had enough to eat! This story reminds us that when we give what we have to God, even if it feels small, He can use it in big ways to bless others.

 **ACTIVITY**

Draw a basket with five loaves and two fish. Write "God provides" on the basket.

PRAYER

Thank You, Jesus, for providing for me. Help me to share what I have with others. Amen.

Chapter 274: Jesus Walks on Water

"Take courage! It is I. Don't be afraid."
- Matthew 14:27

One night, after a long day of teaching, Jesus' disciples were caught in a storm while crossing a lake in their boat. Suddenly, they saw Jesus walking on the water toward them! At first, they were frightened, thinking He was a ghost, but Jesus told them not to be afraid. Peter even tried to walk on water too, but when he looked at the waves, he got scared and started to sink. Jesus caught him and helped him back to the boat. This story shows us that even when life feels stormy, Jesus is always close and ready to help us when we call out to Him.

 ACTIVITY

Use a toy boat in a bowl of water. Make little waves with your hand and imagine Jesus walking on the water!

 PRAYER

Jesus, thank You for helping me when I'm scared. Help me to remember You are always near. Amen.

Chapter 275: The Parable of the Sower

"Still other seed fell on good soil, where it produced a crop." - Matthew 13:8

Jesus told a story about a farmer planting seeds, but not all the seeds grew well. Some fell on hard paths, some on rocky ground, and some among thorns. Only the seeds that landed in good soil grew into healthy plants. This parable teaches us that our hearts need to be like good soil, ready to listen to God's Word, believe it, and live it out. When we keep our hearts soft and open to God, our faith can grow and produce good things, like kindness, love, and obedience.

 ## ACTIVITY

Plant a seed in a cup of dirt. Watch it grow this week and think about growing your faith.

 ## PRAYER

God, help my heart be like good soil. Let Your Word grow in me. Amen.

Chapter 276: The Parable of the Weeds

"Let both grow together until the harvest." – Matthew 13:30

In this parable, Jesus compared God's kingdom to a farmer's field. The farmer planted good seeds, but an enemy secretly planted weeds too. Instead of pulling the weeds right away, the farmer waited until harvest time to separate them. This teaches us that in the world, there will be both good and bad, but God is patient and gives everyone time to change. One day, God will make everything right, but for now, He wants us to focus on growing strong in faith and doing good.

 **ACTIVITY**

Draw a field with wheat and weeds. Talk about how God knows the right time for everything.

PRAYER

God, thank You for being patient. Help me trust Your timing. Amen.

Chapter 277: The Parable of the Mustard Seed

"It is the smallest of all seeds, but when it grows, it is the largest of garden plants." - Matthew 13:32

Jesus said the kingdom of God is like a tiny mustard seed. Though it starts small, it grows into a big tree where birds can rest in its branches. This reminds us that small beginnings can lead to great things when God is in charge. Maybe you feel too small to make a difference, but every prayer, kind word, and act of love plants a seed that God can grow into something amazing.

 ## ACTIVITY

Find the smallest seed or object you can. Put it in your hand and remember: God can grow big things from small beginnings!

 ## PRAYER

Jesus, help my faith to grow, even if it starts small. Amen.

Chapter 278: The Parable of the Leaven

"The kingdom of heaven is like yeast that a woman took and mixed into flour." - Matthew 13:33

In this story, Jesus compared God's kingdom to yeast, which makes dough rise. You can't see the yeast working, but soon the dough gets bigger and fluffy! That's like the way God works in our hearts and in the world. Even small acts of faith, kindness, and love can spread and help others grow closer to God, just like yeast quietly makes bread rise.

 ACTIVITY

Watch bread rise or look at bubbles in soda. Talk about how little things can change big things.

 PRAYER

God, use me to help spread Your love and kindness everywhere. Amen.

Chapter 279: The Parable of the Hidden Treasure

"The kingdom of heaven is like treasure hidden in a field." – Matthew 13:44

Jesus told a story about a man who found treasure buried in a field. He was so excited that he sold everything he had just to buy that field! This reminds us that following Jesus is the greatest treasure we can ever find. It's worth more than toys, money, or anything else because His love lasts forever.

 **ACTIVITY**

Hide a small toy or coin and have a treasure hunt! Remember that knowing Jesus is the greatest treasure.

 **PRAYER**

Jesus, You are my treasure. Help me to love You more than anything else. Amen.

Chapter 280: The Parable of the Pearl

"He went and sold all he had and bought it." - Matthew 13:46

A merchant was searching for pearls and found one so beautiful that he sold everything he had to buy it. Jesus told this story to show us that knowing God is the most precious thing in life. When we follow Jesus, we are choosing something more valuable than anything money can buy: His love, His friendship, and eternal life with Him.

 **ACTIVITY**

Draw a pearl inside a clam shell. Write "Jesus is my treasure" beside it.

PRAYER

Thank You, Jesus, for being the greatest gift. Help me to put You first in my life. Amen.

Chapter 281: The Parable of the Net

"They collected the good fish in baskets, but threw the bad away." - *Matthew 13:48*

Jesus said the kingdom of heaven is like a big fishing net that catches all kinds of fish. Later, the fishermen sort the good fish from the bad. This story reminds us that one day, God will separate those who love and follow Him from those who chose not to. God invites everyone to follow Him now, so we can be part of His forever family.

 **ACTIVITY**

Draw a big fishing net. Inside, draw lots of fish. Color the good fish brightly!

PRAYER

God, help me to follow You and live for Your kingdom. Amen.

Chapter 282: Jesus Heals Many People

"All who touched him were healed." - Mark 6:56

Wherever Jesus went, people brought their sick friends and family to Him. Some were blind, some couldn't walk, and some were very sick in other ways. But Jesus never turned anyone away. He healed them all because He loved them so much. This reminds us that Jesus still cares for us today. When we are sick, sad, or worried, we can come to Him in prayer. Jesus is the Great Healer, and even when healing doesn't happen right away, He promises to be with us and give us comfort and hope.

 **ACTIVITY**

Make a card or draw a picture for someone who is sick to encourage them.

PRAYER

Jesus, thank You for caring about people. Help me to be kind and loving like You. Amen.

Chapter 283: Jesus Teaches About Forgiveness

"Forgive, and you will be forgiven." -
Luke 6:37

Forgiveness is sometimes hard, but Jesus teaches us to forgive others, just like God forgives us. When someone hurts our feelings, it's easy to stay mad, but holding on to anger makes our hearts heavy. Forgiving sets us free from that hurt. Forgiveness doesn't mean pretending nothing happened; it means choosing love instead of staying upset. God forgives us again and again, and He wants us to do the same for others.

 **ACTIVITY**

Think of someone you need to forgive. Write "I forgive you" on a piece of paper as a reminder.

 **PRAYER**

God, thank You for forgiving me. Help me to forgive others from my heart. Amen.

Chapter 284: The Parable of the Unmerciful Servant

"Shouldn't you have had mercy on your fellow servant just as I had on you?" - Matthew 18:33

Jesus told a story about a man who owed a king a huge amount of money. The king forgave him completely! But then that man refused to forgive someone who owed him just a little bit. This parable teaches us that God has forgiven us for so much, so we should forgive others too. Mercy means showing kindness even when someone has done something wrong. When we forgive, we show the world how much God loves.

 **ACTIVITY**

Draw a heart and write the word "MERCY" inside. Think about how to show mercy today.

PRAYER

Jesus, help me remember Your mercy. Teach me to forgive like You do. Amen.

Chapter 285: The Good Samaritan

"Love your neighbor as yourself." - Luke 10:27

When Jesus was asked, "Who is my neighbor?" He told the story of the Good Samaritan. A man was hurt on the road, and while others walked by, a Samaritan stopped to help, even though Samaritans and Jews were usually enemies. Jesus taught that loving our neighbor means helping anyone in need, even if they are different from us. Real love takes action, and kindness is for everyone.

 **ACTIVITY**

Draw two stick people, one helping the other. Talk about how you can be like the Good Samaritan today.

PRAYER

Jesus, help me to love my neighbors and be kind to everyone. Amen.

Chapter 286: Mary and Martha

"Mary has chosen what is better, and it will not be taken away from her." - Luke 10:42

When Jesus visited Mary and Martha, Martha was busy cooking and cleaning while Mary sat and listened to Jesus. Martha got upset, but Jesus gently reminded her that sometimes it's more important to spend time with God than to worry about chores. It's good to work hard, but it's also important to pause, pray, and listen to God. Spending time with Jesus helps us grow in love and faith.

 ACTIVITY

Find a quiet spot and sit still for one minute. Think about Jesus and how much He loves you.

 PRAYER

Jesus, help me remember to spend time with You and not get too busy. Amen.

Chapter 287: The Rich Fool

"Life does not consist in an abundance of possessions." - Luke 12:15

Jesus told a parable about a man who saved up lots of things for himself but forgot about God. He thought life was about getting more and more stuff. But Jesus teaches us that life is about loving God and loving others, not about how many toys or treasures we have. Our relationship with God is the most important thing of all.

 **ACTIVITY**

Draw a treasure chest and write inside it things that matter most, like love, family, and faith.

PRAYER

God, help me to treasure what really matters: knowing You and loving others. Amen.

Chapter 288: The Lost Sheep

"Rejoice with me; I have found my lost sheep." – Luke 15:6

Jesus said He is like a shepherd who searches for one lost sheep until He finds it. Even though the shepherd had 99 other sheep, he left them to find the one that was lost. That's how much God loves each of us! When someone is lost or far from God, He will do everything to bring them back. We are never too far from His love.

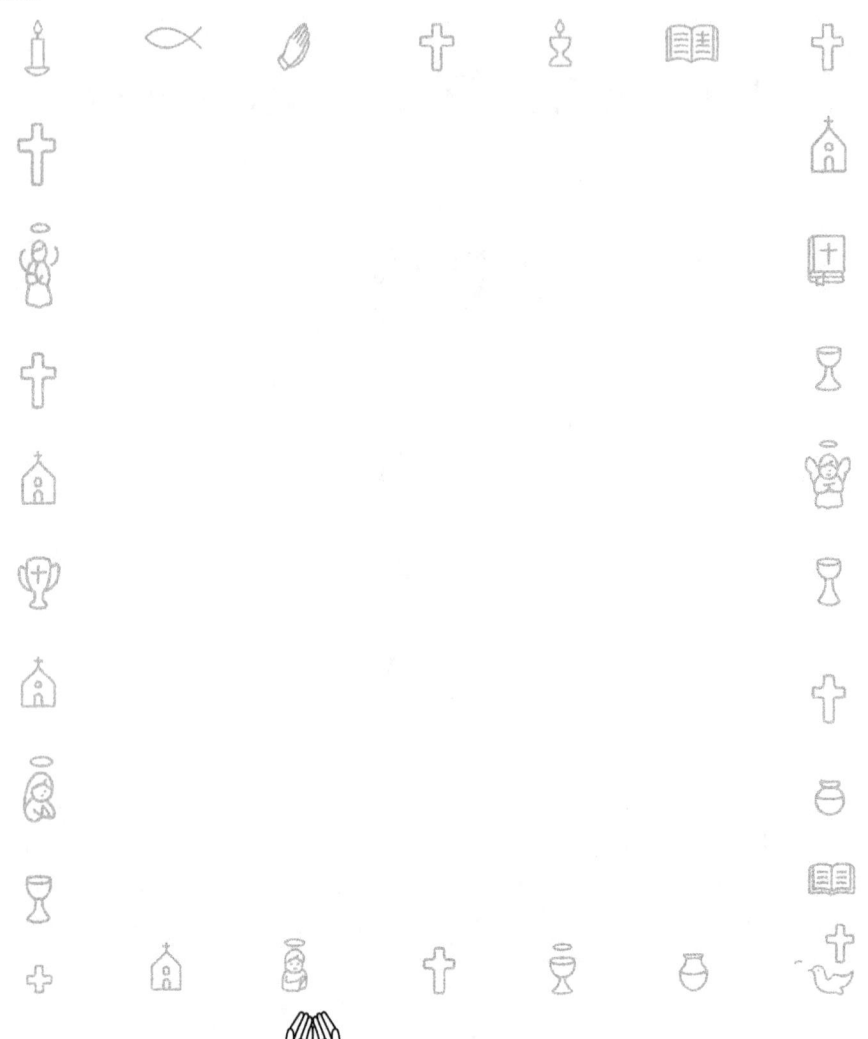

ACTIVITY

Draw a sheep and write your name on it. Remember that Jesus loves you!

PRAYER

Thank You, Jesus, for coming to find me. Help me to always follow You. Amen.

Chapter 289: The Lost Coin

"Rejoice with me; I have found my lost coin." - Luke 15:9

Jesus told a story about a woman who lost one of her ten silver coins. She lit a lamp, swept the whole house, and searched carefully until she found it. Then she was so happy she told her friends! This shows us how much God celebrates when one person chooses to follow Him or returns after wandering away. Each person is precious to God.

 **ACTIVITY**

Hide a coin in your room and try to find it. Celebrate when you do!

 **PRAYER**

God, thank You for loving me so much. Help me to remember that I'm precious to You. Amen.

Chapter 290: The Prodigal Son

"But while he was still a long way off, his father saw him and was filled with compassion." - Luke 15:20

A son left home, spent all his money, and made bad choices. When he finally decided to go back home, his father saw him coming from far away and ran to hug him. The father forgave his son and threw a big party! Jesus told this story to show us that God is always ready to forgive us and welcome us back with open arms, no matter what we've done.

 # ACTIVITY

Draw a picture of a big hug. Remember that God is always ready to welcome you back.

PRAYER

Loving Father, thank You for always forgiving me. Help me to turn back to You whenever I wander. Amen.

Chapter 291: The Rich Man and Lazarus

"Remember that in your lifetime you received your good things, while Lazarus received bad things." - Luke 16:25

Jesus told a story about a rich man who had everything and a poor man named Lazarus who had nothing. After they died, Lazarus was comforted in heaven, and the rich man was sad because he hadn't shared or cared for others. This reminds us to be kind and generous while we have the chance, and to trust in God, not just in things.

 ACTIVITY

Think of one way you can help someone today. Do it with a happy heart.

 PRAYER

Jesus, help me to share and care for others, especially those who need help. Amen.

Chapter 292: The Ten Lepers

"Only one of them came back to say thank you." - Luke 17:15-16

Jesus healed ten men who had leprosy, a sickness that kept them far from their families. But only one came back to thank Jesus. He was so grateful for what Jesus did! This story reminds us to always say thank you to God for the blessings in our lives. Gratitude makes our hearts joyful.

 **ACTIVITY**

Make a list of five things you're thankful for today.

_____

_____

_____

_____

_____

_____

_____

_____

_____

_____

_____

PRAYER

Thank You, Jesus, for all the good things You do. Help me to always be thankful. Amen.

Chapter 293: The Persistent Widow

"Will not God bring about justice for his chosen ones who cry out to him day and night?" - Luke 18:7

Jesus told a story about a widow who kept asking a judge for help until he finally gave her what she needed. She never gave up! Jesus shared this parable to teach us to keep praying and never stop trusting God. Even if the answer doesn't come right away, God hears us and is always working for our good.

 **ACTIVITY**

Write the word "PRAY" and decorate it. Put it where you'll see it and remember to keep praying.

PRAYER

God, thank You for hearing my prayers. Help me to keep talking to You every day. Amen.

Chapter 294: The Pharisee and the Tax Collector

"God, have mercy on me, a sinner." - Luke 18:13

Two men went to the temple to pray. One bragged about how good he was, while the other humbly asked God for forgiveness. Jesus said the humble man was the one God accepted. God loves when we come to Him with honesty and ask for help, not when we try to act like we're better than others.

 **ACTIVITY**

Draw a small heart and a big heart. Write "Be humble" in the small one, to remind you that humility is big in God's eyes.

PRAYER

God, help me to be humble and remember that I need You. Amen.

Chapter 295: Jesus Blesses the Children

"Let the little children come to me." - Mark 10:14

Some people thought children shouldn't bother Jesus, but He said, "Let the children come to me!" Jesus loves kids and wants them to know they are special to Him. You don't have to be a grown-up to have a close relationship with Jesus: He loves you just as you are!

 # ACTIVITY

Draw yourself sitting with Jesus. Imagine talking to Him.

PRAYER

Jesus, thank You for loving me just as I am. Help me to always come close to You. Amen.

Chapter 296: The Rich Young Ruler

"Go, sell everything you have and give to the poor." - Mark 10:21

A rich young man asked Jesus how to follow Him. Jesus told him to give up the things he loved most, his money and stuff, but the man went away sad because he wasn't ready to let go. Jesus wants us to love Him more than anything else. He wants our hearts to be focused on Him, not on things.

 **ACTIVITY**

Think about one thing you can share this week to help someone else.

_____

_____

_____

_____

_____

_____

_____

_____

_____

_____

_____

PRAYER

Jesus, help me to put You first in my life. Teach me to be generous and kind. Amen.

Chapter 297: Zacchaeus Meets Jesus

"Zacchaeus, come down immediately. I must stay at your house today." - *Luke 19:5*

Zacchaeus was a tax collector who climbed a tree to see Jesus because he was too short to see over the crowd. Even though Zacchaeus wasn't liked by many people, Jesus noticed him and chose to spend time with him. After meeting Jesus, Zacchaeus changed his life and became generous and kind. Jesus loves changing hearts!

 **ACTIVITY**

Draw a tree with Zacchaeus in it. Write "Jesus loves everyone" under your drawing.

PRAYER

Thank You, Jesus, for loving me and calling me by name. Help me to follow You. Amen.

Chapter 298: The Parable of the Talents

"Well done, good and faithful servant!" - Matthew 25:23

In this story, a master gave his servants different amounts of money to take care of while he was gone. The servants who used their talents wisely were praised. Jesus wants us to use the gifts He gives us, our time, talents, and kindness, for His glory. When we do, we hear God's smile in our hearts!

 **ACTIVITY**

Make a list of things you're good at or enjoy. How can you use them for God?

_____

_____

_____

_____

_____

_____

_____

_____

_____

PRAYER

God, thank You for the talents You've given me. Help me to use them for You. Amen.

Chapter 299: Jesus Raises Lazarus

"Lazarus, come out!" - John 11:43

Lazarus was Jesus' friend, and when he died, his sisters were very sad. But Jesus showed His power over death by calling Lazarus out of the tomb alive! This miracle reminds us that Jesus has the power to give life and that He is always with us, even in sad times. His love is stronger than anything, even death.

 **ACTIVITY**

Draw a tomb with the stone rolled away. Write "Jesus gives life!" underneath.

PRAYER

Jesus, thank You for being stronger than death. Help me to trust in Your power and love. Amen.

Chapter 300: Jesus Enters Jerusalem

"Blessed is he who comes in the name of the Lord!" - Matthew 21:9

When Jesus rode into Jerusalem on a donkey, people waved palm branches and shouted "Hosanna!" They were celebrating their King. Jesus was a different kind of king: He came humbly, to bring peace and save the world, not to rule with power. We can welcome Jesus as King into our hearts today too.

 ACTIVITY

Make a paper palm branch and wave it while saying "Hosanna!"

 **PRAYER**

Jesus, You are my King. I praise You and welcome You into my heart. Amen.

Chapter 301: Jesus Cleanses the Temple Again

"My house will be called a house of prayer." - Matthew 21:13

When Jesus went to the temple in Jerusalem, He saw people selling animals and exchanging money right there in the place meant for worship. He became very upset because the temple was supposed to be a special place to talk to God, not a marketplace. Jesus flipped over the tables and told everyone to leave. This reminds us that God wants our hearts to be like a clean temple: a place of love, prayer, and kindness, not selfishness or greed.

 **ACTIVITY**

Draw a simple church and write "House of Prayer" above it. Think about ways you can make your heart a peaceful place for God.

PRAYER

God, help me to worship You with a clean and loving heart. Teach me to honor You every day. Amen.

Chapter 302: The Greatest Commandment

"Love the Lord your God... and love your neighbor as yourself." - Matthew 22:37-39

When someone asked Jesus what the most important rule was, He gave a beautiful answer: Love God with all your heart, and love others like you love yourself. Jesus wants us to know that loving God and loving people is more important than anything else. When we love this way, we follow God's greatest plan for our lives.

 **ACTIVITY**

Draw two hearts. Label one "Love God" and the other "Love Others." Think of one way you can do both today.

 **PRAYER**

Jesus, help me to love You with all my heart and love other people too. Amen.

Chapter 303: The Widow's Offering

"She put in all she had to live on." - Luke 21:4

At the temple, rich people gave lots of money, but a poor widow gave just two tiny coins. Jesus said she gave more than anyone else because she gave from her heart, not just from her leftover money. God cares more about our love and trust than the size of our gifts. Even when we give something small, if it's given with love, God smiles.

 ACTIVITY

Draw two small coins and write "Give with love" under them.

PRAYER

God, help me to give cheerfully and trust You to take care of me. Amen.

Chapter 304: The Signs of the End Times

"Be always on the watch, and pray." - Luke 21:36

Jesus told His disciples about things that would happen in the world before He comes back someday, like wars, earthquakes, and other troubles. He also said not to be afraid. Jesus told us to be ready and to keep trusting God, knowing that He will make everything right in the end. We don't know when He will return, but we can live each day loving God and loving others.

 **ACTIVITY**

Draw a clock or a watch. Write "Be ready!" next to it.

PRAYER

Jesus, help me to live for You every day and be ready for Your return.
Amen.

Chapter 305: The Parable of the Ten Virgins

"The bridegroom came, and those who were ready went in with him." -
Matthew 25:10

Jesus told a story about ten girls waiting for a wedding. Some brought extra oil for their lamps, but others did not. When the bridegroom came, only the ones who were prepared could go in. This teaches us to always be ready for Jesus, keeping our hearts close to Him and living the way He wants us to.

 **ACTIVITY**

Draw a lamp and color it bright. Write "Be ready" on it to remind yourself to stay close to God.

PRAYER

Jesus, help me to keep my heart ready for You every day. Amen.

Chapter 306: The Parable of the Sheep and Goats

"Whatever you did for one of the least of these brothers and sisters of mine, you did for me." - Matthew 25:40

Jesus told a story about a shepherd separating sheep from goats. The sheep were people who loved others by feeding the hungry, helping the sick, and caring for the lonely. Jesus said that when we help others, it's like we're helping Him. God wants us to serve others with love and kindness every day.

 **ACTIVITY**

Think of one kind thing you can do for someone today. Do it with joy!

 **PRAYER**

Jesus, help me to see You in other people and love them like You do. Amen.

Chapter 307: Jesus Predicts His Death

"The Son of Man will be delivered over to be crucified." - Matthew 26:2

Jesus told His disciples that He would soon die on the cross, but they didn't understand why. Jesus knew it was part of God's plan to save the world. He loved us so much that He was willing to suffer for our sins so we could have new life. This shows us how deep and powerful His love is.

 **ACTIVITY**

Draw a cross and write "Thank You, Jesus" underneath.

PRAYER

Jesus, thank You for loving me enough to give Your life for me. Help me to remember Your great love. Amen.

Chapter 308: Anointing of Jesus

"She poured perfume on my body to prepare me for burial." - Matthew 26:12

Before Jesus died, a woman showed Him great love by pouring expensive perfume on His feet. Some people thought she was wasting it, but Jesus said she had done something beautiful to prepare Him for what was coming. This story reminds us that worship is about giving our best to God, no matter what others think.

 **ACTIVITY**

Draw a bottle of perfume. Write "Worship Jesus" under it.

PRAYER

Jesus, help me to give You my best and love You with all my heart. Amen.

Chapter 309: Judas Agrees to Betray Jesus

"What are you willing to give me if I deliver him over to you?" - Matthew 26:15

Judas, one of Jesus' disciples, made a very sad choice. He agreed to betray Jesus for 30 silver coins. Even though Judas made this terrible decision, Jesus still loved him. This teaches us that God knows everything about us, even our mistakes, and He still offers love and forgiveness.

 **ACTIVITY**

Think about why it's important to make good choices. Talk about it with someone you trust.

 **PRAYER**

Jesus, help me make choices that honor You. Thank You for loving me no matter what. Amen.

Chapter 310: Preparing for Passover

"The Teacher says: My appointed time is near." - Matthew 26:18

Jesus asked His disciples to prepare a special meal called the Passover. This was the last supper Jesus would eat with them before going to the cross. He wanted to spend time with His friends, teach them, and remind them of His love. Today, we still remember this meal when we take communion at church.

 ACTIVITY

Set the table for a meal and remember how Jesus shared His love at the Last Supper.

 **PRAYER**

Jesus, thank You for loving me and giving me the gift of remembering You. Help me to follow You always. Amen.

Chapter 311: The Last Supper

"While they were eating, Jesus took bread, and when he had given thanks, he broke it and gave it to his disciples, saying, 'Take and eat; this is my body.'"
- Matthew 26:26

At the Last Supper, Jesus shared a special meal with His disciples. He took bread and broke it, saying it was like His body, and He shared a cup of juice, saying it was like His blood. Jesus wanted His friends to remember that He was about to give His life to save them. Even today, when Christians take communion, they remember this moment and thank Jesus for His great love and sacrifice.

 **ACTIVITY**

Have a simple meal with your family. Break bread or share a snack together, and talk about how Jesus loves us so much He gave His life for us.

 **PRAYER**

Jesus, thank You for giving Your life for me. Help me to always remember Your love. Amen.

Chapter 312: Jesus Washes His Disciples' Feet

"Now that I, your Lord and Teacher, have washed your feet, you also should wash one another's feet." - John 13:14

At the Last Supper, Jesus did something surprising: He washed His disciples' feet! Back then, people's feet got dirty from walking in sandals all day, and only servants washed feet. But Jesus, the Son of God, wanted to show His friends how to be humble and serve others with love. He teaches us that greatness comes from helping others, not just being first.

 ACTIVITY

Think of one way you can serve someone today, like helping clean up or doing something kind without being asked.

 **PRAYER**

Jesus, thank You for teaching me to be humble and serve others. Help me to love people like You do. Amen.

Chapter 313: Jesus Predicts Peter's Denial

"Truly I tell you," Jesus answered, "this very night, before the rooster crows, you will disown me three times." - Matthew 26:34

Jesus told Peter that before the rooster crowed in the morning, Peter would say three times that he didn't know Jesus. Peter loved Jesus very much, but when things got scary, he made a mistake and denied knowing Him. Jesus still loved Peter and forgave him later. This reminds us that Jesus loves us even when we mess up and is always ready to forgive us when we say we're sorry.

 **ACTIVITY**

Think about a time you made a mistake. Talk to God about it, and thank Him for forgiving you.

 **PRAYER**

Forgiving Jesus, thank You for loving me even when I fail. Help me to trust You and to forgive others too. Amen.

Chapter 314: Jesus Prays in the Garden

"Father, if you are willing, take this cup from me; yet not my will, but yours be done." - Luke 22:42

Before going to the cross, Jesus prayed in a garden called Gethsemane. He knew what was going to happen, and it made Him sad and afraid. But He chose to obey God because He loved us so much. Jesus teaches us to pray honestly to God about our feelings and to trust God's plan, even when it's hard.

 ## ACTIVITY

Find a quiet place to pray today. Talk to God about something that worries you. Trust that He will help you.

 ## PRAYER

Father God, thank You for hearing my prayers. Help me to trust You, just like Jesus did in the garden. Amen.

Chapter 315: Jesus Is Arrested

"Then the men stepped forward, seized Jesus and arrested him." - Matthew 26:50

After Jesus prayed, soldiers came to arrest Him. One of His disciples, Judas, betrayed Him by leading the soldiers to Him. Even though Jesus could have stopped them, because He had the power of God, He let it happen because He knew it was part of God's plan to rescue the world from sin. Jesus chose love, even when it was hard.

 **ACTIVITY**

Think about a time you felt left out or hurt by someone. Remember that Jesus understands those feelings and is with you.

 **PRAYER**

Jesus, thank You for choosing love, even when it was hard. Help me to follow You and love others too. Amen.

Chapter 316: Peter Denies Jesus

"Immediately a rooster crowed. Then Peter remembered the word Jesus had spoken." - Matthew 26:74-75

When Jesus was arrested, Peter was scared. Just like Jesus said, Peter told people three times that he didn't know Jesus. When the rooster crowed, Peter felt very sad and cried. Later, Jesus forgave him and welcomed him back as a friend and leader. Jesus forgives us too, no matter how big or small our mistakes are.

 **ACTIVITY**

Write the word "FORGIVEN" on a piece of paper and decorate it. Keep it somewhere to remind you of God's love.

PRAYER

Jesus, thank You for forgiving me when I make mistakes. Help me to be brave and stay close to You. Amen.

Chapter 317: Jesus Before Pilate

"Pilate asked, 'What shall I do, then, with Jesus who is called the Messiah?' They all answered, 'Crucify him!'" - Matthew 27:22

Jesus was taken to Pilate, the Roman governor. Pilate knew Jesus had done nothing wrong, but he listened to the crowd instead of standing up for what was right. They shouted, "Crucify Him!" and Pilate gave in. Sometimes doing the right thing is hard, but God wants us to be brave and stand up for truth.

 ACTIVITY

Talk with someone about a time when you had to make a hard choice to do the right thing. What helped you be brave?

 PRAYER

Jesus, help me to stand up for what is right, even when it's hard. Thank You for loving me no matter what. Amen.

Chapter 318: Jesus Is Crucified

"When they came to the place called the Skull, they crucified him there."
- Luke 23:33

Jesus was nailed to a cross, even though He had never done anything wrong. He chose to take the punishment for our sins because He loves us. On the cross, Jesus showed the greatest love the world has ever seen. He died so that we could be forgiven and live forever with Him one day.

 **ACTIVITY**

Draw a cross and inside it write or draw pictures of things you are thankful for because of Jesus' love.

PRAYER

Jesus, thank You for dying on the cross for me. Help me to remember Your love every day. Amen.

Chapter 319: The Death of Jesus

"Jesus called out with a loud voice, 'Father, into your hands I commit my spirit.'" - Luke 23:46

When Jesus died on the cross, He finished the work of saving us from sin. The sky turned dark, and the earth shook. It was a sad moment, but also a moment of victory because Jesus' death opened the way for us to be close to God again. Jesus gave His life because He loves you so much.

 **ACTIVITY**

Sit quietly for one minute, thinking about how much Jesus loves you. Then say "Thank You, Jesus."

 **PRAYER**

Jesus, thank You for giving Your life for me. Help me to love You more each day. Amen.

Chapter 320: Jesus Is Buried

"Then he rolled a stone against the entrance of the tomb." - Mark 15:46

Jesus' friends placed His body in a tomb, and a huge stone was rolled in front of it. They were very sad and didn't understand what would happen next.

God had a wonderful surprise coming! Even when life feels dark or sad, we can trust that God is always working for good.

 ## ACTIVITY

Find a small rock and hold it in your hand. Imagine the big stone in front of Jesus' tomb, and remember that God always has a plan.

 ## PRAYER

God, thank You that the story doesn't end in sadness. Help me to trust that You always have a plan. Amen.

Chapter 321: The Empty Tomb

"He is not here; he has risen, just as he said." - Matthew 28:6

On the third day after Jesus died, His friends went to His tomb, but they found the stone rolled away and the tomb empty! An angel told them the good news: Jesus was alive! This is why we celebrate Easter, because Jesus rose from the dead. He defeated sin and death so that we can have new life with Him forever. His resurrection shows us that with God, nothing is impossible.

 **ACTIVITY**

Draw an empty tomb with light shining out of it. Say, "Jesus is alive!" three times with a happy heart.

PRAYER

Thank You, Jesus, for rising from the dead! I am so happy that You are alive. Amen.

Chapter 322: Mary Magdalene Sees Jesus

"She turned toward him and cried out in Aramaic, 'Rabboni!' (which means Teacher)." - John 20:16

Mary Magdalene was crying at the empty tomb because she thought someone had taken Jesus' body. Then, Jesus appeared to her and said her name. Right away, she knew it was Him! Jesus cares about each of us personally and knows our names too. He wants us to know Him as our loving Savior and friend.

 **ACTIVITY**

Write your name on a piece of paper. Say out loud, "Jesus knows my name and loves me."

 **PRAYER**

Jesus, thank You for knowing my name and loving me. Help me to listen for Your voice every day. Amen.

Chapter 323: On the Road to Emmaus

"Then their eyes were opened and they recognized him." - Luke 24:31

Two of Jesus' friends were walking to a village called Emmaus, feeling sad because Jesus had died. As they walked, Jesus joined them, but they didn't recognize Him at first. Later, when He broke bread with them, they realized who He was! This story reminds us that sometimes Jesus is working in our lives, even when we don't see Him right away.

 **ACTIVITY**

Draw two people walking on a path with Jesus beside them. Remember that He walks with you too.

PRAYER

Jesus, help me to see You and know You better every day. Thank You for walking with me. Amen.

Chapter 324: Jesus Appears to His Disciples

"Peace be with you." - John 20:19

Jesus appeared to His disciples after He rose from the dead. They were scared and hiding, but Jesus came to them and said, "Peace be with you." He showed them His hands and His side so they would know it was really Him. Jesus gives us peace when we are afraid and reminds us that He is always with us.

 **ACTIVITY**

Put your hand on your heart and take a deep breath. Imagine Jesus saying, "Peace be with you."

 **PRAYER**

Jesus, thank You for bringing peace to my heart. Help me not to be afraid because You are alive. Amen.

Chapter 325: Thomas Believes

"Stop doubting and believe." - John 20:27

Thomas wasn't with the other disciples when Jesus first appeared to them, and he said he wouldn't believe unless he saw Jesus himself. Later, Jesus came to Thomas and showed him His scars. Thomas believed right away and said, "My Lord and my God!" Jesus loves us even when we have questions, and He helps us believe.

 **ACTIVITY**

Think about something you have doubted before. Write "I believe!" on a piece of paper.

 **PRAYER**

Jesus, thank You for helping me believe. Help me to trust You, even when I don't understand everything. Amen.

Chapter 326: Jesus Appears by the Sea

"Jesus said to them, 'Come and have breakfast.'" - John 21:12

One morning, Jesus' friends were fishing but couldn't catch anything. Then Jesus appeared on the shore and told them where to throw their nets. They caught so many fish they could hardly pull them in! When they came to shore, Jesus made them breakfast. This story shows us that Jesus cares about every part of our lives, even small things like breakfast!

 **ACTIVITY**

Have breakfast or a snack and imagine Jesus sitting beside you. What would you say to Him?

 **PRAYER**

Jesus, thank You for being with me in everyday moments. Help me to always remember You are near. Amen.

Chapter 327: Jesus Gives Instructions

"Go into all the world and preach the gospel to all creation." - Mark 16:15

Before Jesus went back to heaven, He gave His friends a big job: to tell the whole world about His love. This is called the Great Commission. We can help share Jesus' love too, by telling others about Him, showing kindness, and living like Jesus.

 **ACTIVITY**

Draw the earth. Inside it, write or draw ways you can share Jesus' love with others.

PRAYER

Jesus, help me to tell others about You. Give me courage to share Your love everywhere I go. Amen.

Chapter 328: The Great Commission

"Therefore go and make disciples of all nations." - Matthew 28:19

Jesus wants us to share His story with everyone, near and far. Making disciples means helping people learn about Jesus and follow Him too. We do this by living in a way that shows love, teaching others about God, and helping them grow in faith.

 **ACTIVITY**

Think of one person you can pray for today who needs to know Jesus. Say a prayer for them now.

 **PRAYER**

Jesus, thank You for trusting me to share Your good news. Help me be bold and loving as I tell others about You. Amen.

Chapter 329: Jesus Ascends to Heaven

"He was taken up before their very eyes, and a cloud hid him from their sight." - Acts 1:9

After teaching His friends for 40 days, Jesus went back to heaven. He promised to return someday, but until then, He is always with us through His Spirit. Jesus is preparing a special place for us in heaven, and one day, we will be with Him forever!

 **ACTIVITY**

Look at the sky today and imagine Jesus watching over you from heaven. Wave hello to Him!

 **PRAYER**

Jesus, thank You for going to heaven to prepare a place for me. Help me to live for You while I wait for Your return. Amen.

Chapter 330: Waiting for the Holy Spirit

"But you will receive power when the Holy Spirit comes on you." - Acts 1:8

Before Jesus went to heaven, He told His disciples to wait for the Holy Spirit. The Holy Spirit would come to help them be brave and share God's love with the world. Today, the Holy Spirit lives in us too, giving us strength, courage, and guidance. We are never alone: God's Spirit is always with us!

 ## ACTIVITY

Close your eyes and take a deep breath. Imagine God's Spirit filling you with love and courage.

 ## PRAYER

Holy Spirit, thank You for living in me. Help me to be brave and kind as I follow Jesus. Amen.

Chapter 331: The Holy Spirit Comes

"All of them were filled with the Holy Spirit." - Acts 2:4

On the day of Pentecost, Jesus' followers were praying together when suddenly a loud sound like wind filled the room, and little flames appeared over their heads. They were filled with the Holy Spirit and began to speak in different languages! This was the beginning of the church. The Holy Spirit gave them courage and power to tell others about Jesus. Today, the Holy Spirit still fills us with love, strength, and boldness to live for God.

 **ACTIVITY**

Draw a picture of wind and flames. Say, "Holy Spirit, fill me with Your love."

PRAYER

Holy Spirit, thank You for coming into my life. Help me to share Jesus with others. Amen.

Chapter 332: Peter Preaches About Jesus

"Repent and be baptized, every one of you." - Acts 2:38

After receiving the Holy Spirit, Peter stood up in front of a huge crowd and told them about Jesus. Even though Peter had once denied Jesus, now he was bold and brave. Peter explained how Jesus died and rose again to save us. Many people believed that day and were baptized. God can use each of us to share His message when we trust Him.

 **ACTIVITY**

Pretend you're giving a short speech. Practice telling someone, "Jesus loves you and wants to be your friend!"

 **PRAYER**

Jesus, thank You for giving me courage like Peter. Help me to tell others about You. Amen.

Chapter 333: The Early Church Shares Everything

"They shared everything they had." - Acts 2:44

After the Holy Spirit came, the new believers shared their homes, food, and money. They took care of each other so no one would go without. They prayed together, ate together, and loved one another. This is how Jesus wants His followers to live: sharing and caring, like one big family.

 **ACTIVITY**

Share something today, like a toy or snack, with a happy heart.

 **PRAYER**

Jesus, help me to share and care for others like the first church did. Thank You for loving me. Amen.

Chapter 334: Healing at the Temple Gate

"In the name of Jesus Christ of Nazareth, walk." - Acts 3:6

One day, Peter and John went to the temple to pray. At the gate, they saw a man who had never been able to walk. He was begging for money because he couldn't work.

Peter said, "I don't have silver or gold, but I will give you what I have. In the name of Jesus, walk!" Immediately, the man's legs became strong, and he started walking, jumping, and praising God! Everyone who saw it was amazed. This miracle showed that Jesus' power is real and that God cares about each person's needs.

 **ACTIVITY**

Jump up and down like the healed man and shout, "Thank You, Jesus!"

 **PRAYER**

Jesus, thank You for healing hearts and bodies. Help me to trust You for everything I need. Amen.

Chapter 335: Stephen, a Brave Witness

"But Stephen, full of the Holy Spirit, looked up to heaven and saw the glory of God." - Acts 7:55

Stephen was one of the first people in the early church chosen to serve others. He was full of the Holy Spirit and loved teaching people about Jesus. Some people didn't like what Stephen was saying, and they became angry. Even when they hurt him, Stephen stayed brave. He forgave them and prayed for them just like Jesus did on the cross. Stephen reminds us to be faithful and bold when sharing God's love, even if it's hard. He trusted God completely and looked up to heaven with peace in his heart.

 **ACTIVITY**

Draw a smiling face looking up at the sky. Write "Be brave for Jesus" next to it.

PRAYER

God, help me to be brave like Stephen. Fill me with courage to share Your love and forgive others. Amen.

Chapter 336: Philip and the Ethiopian

"Then Philip began with that very passage of Scripture and told him the good news about Jesus." - Acts 8:35

Philip was a follower of Jesus who listened carefully when God spoke to him. One day, God told Philip to go to a desert road. There, Philip met an important man from Ethiopia who was reading the Bible but didn't understand it. Philip explained the Scriptures and told him all about Jesus. The man was so happy that he believed in Jesus and was baptized right away. This story teaches us that God can use us to help others learn about Him, even in surprising places.

 ACTIVITY

Pretend you're explaining a Bible verse to a friend or family member. Practice telling the good news!

 **PRAYER**

Jesus, help me to listen when You guide me. Show me how to tell others about You. Amen.

Chapter 337: Saul's Conversion

"Saul, Saul, why do you persecute me?" - Acts 9:4

Saul did not believe in Jesus at first. In fact, he tried to stop Jesus' followers from teaching others about God's love. One day, while Saul was traveling on the road to Damascus, a bright light from heaven flashed around him, and he fell to the ground. He heard Jesus' voice asking, "Saul, why are you hurting me?" From that moment, Saul's life changed forever. He realized Jesus was real and decided to follow Him. Later, Saul became known as Paul and spent his life telling the world about Jesus. His story reminds us that no one is too far from God to be forgiven and changed.

 **ACTIVITY**

Draw a picture of Saul seeing the bright light on the road. Write, "Jesus changes hearts" underneath.

PRAYER

Jesus, thank You for loving me and changing lives. Help me follow You with my whole heart. Amen.

Chapter 338: Peter and Cornelius

"God does not show favoritism but accepts from every nation the one who fears him and does what is right." - Acts 10:34-35

Cornelius was a kind Roman soldier who prayed to God and gave to people in need. One day, an angel told Cornelius to send for Peter. At the same time, God gave Peter a vision to teach him that His love is for everyone, not just for one group of people. When Peter visited Cornelius, he shared the story of Jesus with him and his family. They all believed in Jesus and received the Holy Spirit! This story shows us that God welcomes people from every nation, language, and background into His family.

 **ACTIVITY**

Draw a group of people from different places around the world. Write "God loves everyone" above them.

 **PRAYER**

God, thank You for loving everyone, no matter where they are from. Help me to love others like You do. Amen.

Chapter 339: The Good News for Everyone

"Go into all the world and preach the gospel to all creation." - Mark 16:15

Jesus wants everyone to hear the good news of His love! The story of Jesus isn't just for people who live near us, it's for the whole world. That's why His followers traveled far and wide to tell others about God's love. Today, people still share the gospel in different countries, languages, and places. You can help by telling your friends about Jesus or praying for missionaries who go to new places.

 **ACTIVITY**

Draw a globe or a map. Write "Jesus loves the whole world" around it.

PRAYER

Jesus, thank You that Your love is for everyone. Help me to share Your good news with others. Amen.

Chapter 340: Paul's Missionary Journeys

"Go and make disciples of all nations." - Matthew 28:19

Paul traveled on long journeys to tell people about Jesus. Sometimes he went by boat, sometimes by foot, and sometimes he faced danger, but he never gave up! He visited cities, started churches, and wrote letters to encourage believers. Paul's journeys helped spread the message of Jesus to the world. We can follow his example by sharing God's love wherever we go.

 # ACTIVITY

Draw a path or a map with arrows showing travel. Write "Share Jesus everywhere" on it.

PRAYER

God, help me to go where You send me and tell others about Your love. Amen.

Chapter 341: Paul and Silas in Prison

"About midnight Paul and Silas were praying and singing hymns to God." - Acts 16:25

Paul and Silas were put in prison for telling people about Jesus. Instead of being sad, they sang songs and prayed! God sent an earthquake that opened the prison doors, but Paul and Silas stayed to tell the jailer about Jesus. The jailer and his whole family became believers! This story teaches us that we can praise God no matter what and that God can turn hard times into moments of joy.

 **ACTIVITY**

Sing a worship song today like Paul and Silas did in prison.

 **PRAYER**

Jesus, thank You for being with me in good times and hard times. Help me to praise You always. Amen.

Chapter 342: Lydia, a Believer

"The Lord opened her heart to respond to Paul's message." - Acts 16:14

Lydia was a businesswoman who sold purple cloth. When Paul shared the message of Jesus, Lydia listened carefully. God opened her heart, and she believed in Jesus! Lydia was baptized, and she invited Paul and his friends to stay in her home. Her story shows us that when we listen to God, He helps us grow in faith and share His love with others.

 **ACTIVITY**

Draw a purple heart and write "I believe in Jesus" inside it.

PRAYER

God, help me to listen to You and share Your love like Lydia did. Amen.

Chapter 343: Living by the Spirit

"Since we live by the Spirit, let us keep in step with the Spirit." - Galatians 5:25

When we follow Jesus, the Holy Spirit lives in us and helps us live the way God wants. Living by the Spirit means choosing love, kindness, and goodness every day. Sometimes it's hard, but the Spirit gives us strength. When we walk with God, we grow to be more like Jesus.

 **ACTIVITY**

Take a walk and imagine walking step by step with Jesus.

 **PRAYER**

Holy Spirit, help me to live in a way that makes You happy. Guide me every day. Amen.

Chapter 344: The Fruit of the Spirit: Love

"Love one another as I have loved you." - John 15:12

Love is the Spirit's signature on every Christian life: a choice to reach out with kindness, patience, and compassion, even when it costs us. Jesus made that love visible by laying down His life for us, showing how far God will go to bridge the gap between heaven and earth. When we step in to help someone who's hurting, offer forgiveness to someone who's wronged us, or speak words of encouragement to a friend in need, we mirror the same self-giving heart of Christ and let Hi

 ## ACTIVITY

Draw a big red heart and write "Love" in the middle. Think of one loving thing you can do today.

PRAYER

Jesus, help me to love others like You love me. Amen.

Chapter 345: The Fruit of the Spirit: Joy

"The joy of the Lord is your strength." - Nehemiah 8:10

Real joy goes deeper than a passing mood: it springs from knowing deep in your heart that nothing can separate you from God's love. When life feels heavy, this joy is like an unshakable anchor, holding you steady and giving you the strength to keep going. It bubbles up in laughter, fuels your hope in hard moments, and spills out through acts of kindness and words of encouragement. Let this lasting joy be your hidden power: lifting your spirit, brightening your days, and sharing light wherever you go.

 ACTIVITY

Draw a smiley face and write "Joy" above it. Tell someone one thing that makes you joyful.

PRAYER

God, thank You for filling my heart with joy. Help me to share joy with others. Amen.

Chapter 346: The Fruit of the Spirit: Peace

"Let the peace of Christ rule in your hearts." - Colossians 3:15

When Christ's peace takes the lead in our minds, it keeps us steady amid life's rush and noise. This is an inner calm that stands firm because we know He holds every tomorrow. As we carry that settled confidence into our homes, classrooms, and friendships, our calm presence can soothe worries, encourage others, and point people back to the One who offers peace no matter what storms swirl around us.

 **ACTIVITY**

Close your eyes, take a deep breath, and say, "Thank You, God, for Your peace."

 **PRAYER**

Jesus, thank You for giving me peace. Help me to be a peacemaker. Amen.

Chapter 347: The Fruit of the Spirit: Patience

"Be patient, bearing with one another in love." - Ephesians 4:2

Patience is choosing calm trust instead of grumbling when things move at their own pace. It's resisting the urge to rush ahead and instead leaning into kindness when others stumble or hold us up. Because God is endlessly patient with us, even when we mess up or lag behind. He invites us to echo that same long-suffering grace toward friends, family, and even strangers.

When you feel frustration rising, try this simple step: take a deep breath, remind yourself that "God's timing is perfect," and look for one small way to encourage someone else in the wait. Every moment you choose a gentle heart over a hasty complaint, you're not only honoring others, you're deepening your own trust in God's steady love and growing stronger in faith.

 **ACTIVITY**

Think of one thing you're waiting for. Practice being patient today without grumbling.

 **PRAYER**

God, help me to be patient and trust Your timing. Amen.

Chapter 348: The Fruit of the Spirit: Kindness

"Be kind and compassionate to one another." - Ephesians 4:32

Kindness is showing love through our actions and words. It can be as simple as a smile, a hug, or a kind word. Jesus was kind to everyone, and He wants us to be kind too. When we choose kindness, we make the world a better place.

Even the smallest act, like sharing your snack, helping someone up when they fall, or listening when a friend feels sad, can spark a chain reaction of care. Kindness is like throwing a pebble into a pond: the ripples spread farther than we can see. By looking for simple ways to bless others each day, we shine Jesus' light into the world and remind people they're loved.

 ACTIVITY

Do one kind thing for someone today, like helping them or giving a compliment.

 **PRAYER**

Jesus, help me to be kind every day. Show me ways to help others. Amen.

Chapter 349: The Fruit of the Spirit: Goodness

"Do good to all people." - *Galatians 6:10*

Goodness is doing what's right and making choices that please God. When we are good, we act in ways that are honest, fair, and helpful. Goodness means caring about what's right, even when no one is watching.

True goodness shows itself in everyday moments: offering a hand without being asked, speaking up for someone who can't speak for themselves, and choosing honesty even when it's easier to stay quiet. Each small act of integrity helps others see God's heart and builds a world where kindness and justice flourish.

 ACTIVITY

Think of one good deed you can do today. Then go and do it!

 **PRAYER**

God, help me to choose goodness and live in a way that makes You proud. Amen.

Chapter 350: The Fruit of the Spirit: Faithfulness

"Well done, good and faithful servant!"
- Matthew 25:23

Faithfulness means keeping your word, speaking truthfully, and staying devoted to God in every situation. When we live faithfully, people learn they can count on us, and our integrity becomes a powerful witness to God's trustworthiness.

You can grow in faithfulness by practicing simple, daily habits: follow through on small promises, finish tasks even when they're hard, and spend regular time reading God's Word and praying. As you consistently choose what's right, rather than what's easy, your faithfulness becomes a strong foundation, helping others feel secure in your care and pointing them toward the One who is faithful forever.

 ACTIVITY

Write the word "FAITHFUL" on a piece of paper and think of one way to keep a promise today.

 PRAYER

God, thank You for being faithful to me. Help me to be faithful too. Amen.

Chapter 351: The Fruit of the Spirit: Gentleness

"Let your gentleness be evident to all."
- Philippians 4:5

Gentleness is being kind and soft with our words and actions. It's choosing to speak calmly instead of yelling, or helping someone without being rough. Jesus was gentle, and He wants us to be gentle too.

Gentleness also shows up when we listen carefully, giving others space to share, and when we respond with care instead of reacting in anger. By pausing to think about how our words will land and offering a gentle touch or a comforting word, we help people feel safe and valued. Practicing these small acts of tenderness can turn a tense moment into an opportunity for grace.

 **ACTIVITY**

Practice speaking in a soft, gentle voice today. Think of one way to show gentleness.

 **PRAYER**

Jesus, help me to be gentle with others and show love through my actions. Amen.

Chapter 352: The Fruit of the Spirit: Self-Control

"Like a city whose walls are broken through is a person who lacks self-control." - Proverbs 25:28

Self-control means choosing to do what's right, even when you feel like doing something wrong. It's stopping to think before you act or speak. God helps us have self-control so we can make good choices and avoid trouble.

When you feel anger rising or want to take a short-cut to complete a task, pause and take a deep breath. Ask God for strength, count to ten, or even step away for a moment. Practicing these small pauses trains your "self-control muscle," so each time you choose wisely, you grow stronger and better able to handle bigger challenges.

 ## ACTIVITY

Think of one thing that's hard for you to control (like getting angry or eating too much candy). Practice self-control today.

 ## PRAYER

God, help me to have self-control. Teach me to make good choices. Amen.

Chapter 353: What Is Prayer?

"Pray without ceasing." - 1 Thessalonians 5:17

Prayer is talking to God. You can pray anytime, anywhere! You don't have to use fancy words. You can thank God, ask for help, or just tell Him how you feel. Prayer helps you grow closer to God and reminds you that He's always with you.

As you build your prayer life, look for answers in everyday moments: a kind word from a friend when you asked for courage, a sudden idea that helps you solve a problem, or a quiet sense of peace when you felt anxious. You can keep a "prayer journal" to jot down requests and note how God comes through. Over time, you'll see a trail of His faithfulness that encourages you to pray with confidence and joy.

 **ACTIVITY**

Write down one thing you want to talk to God about today. Then pray!

_____

_____

_____

_____

_____

_____

_____

_____

_____

PRAYER

God, thank You for always listening to me. Help me remember to talk to You every day. Amen.

Chapter 354: Why We Pray

"Cast all your anxiety on him because he cares for you." - 1 Peter 5:7

We pray because God loves us and wants to hear from us. When we pray, we give our worries to God and trust Him to help us. Prayer is also a way to thank God for the good things in our lives. He wants to be part of everything we do!

Each time we bring our thoughts to God, we learn to trust His timing and care, even if we don't see answers right away. Talking with Him daily shapes our hearts to match His, teaches us to listen for His voice, and builds a friendship that carries us through every moment.

 ACTIVITY

Think of one thing you're thankful for and one thing you need help with. Pray about both.

 **PRAYER**

Jesus, thank You for caring about me. Help me to trust You with my worries and joys. Amen.

Chapter 355: How to Pray

"This, then, is how you should pray." - Matthew 6:9

Jesus taught His disciples how to pray using the Lord's Prayer. He said to begin by praising God, asking for what we need, saying sorry for mistakes, and forgiving others. We don't have to use perfect words, God just wants to hear our hearts.

You can use the Lord's Prayer as a simple template for your own conversations with God: start by adoring who He is, then lift up your needs, admit where you've gone wrong, choose to forgive others, and close by committing to follow His will. Practicing this pattern helps you focus your thoughts, opens your heart to God's work, and reminds you that prayer is both talking and listening: an ongoing friendship with Him.

 **ACTIVITY**

Write or say your own simple prayer using this pattern: Praise, Ask, Say Sorry, Thank You.

PRAYER

Our Father in heaven, thank You for loving me. Please help me today. Forgive my sins and help me forgive others. Amen.

Chapter 356: Praying for Others

"Pray for each other." - James 5:16

Praying for others is a heartfelt way to show we care. We can lift up friends, family members, teachers, or anyone who feels lonely, worried, or unwell. God listens to every request we bring on behalf of someone else, and He delights when we intercede for those in need.

A simple way to practice this is to keep a "prayer list" where you write down names and specific requests. Each day, pick one person from your list to pray for, asking God to give them peace, strength, or healing. Over time, you'll see how prayer connects your heart to others and invites God to work in their lives.

 **ACTIVITY**

Make a prayer list of people you want to pray for. Pray for each one by name.

_____

_____

_____

_____

_____

_____

_____

_____

_____

_____

_____

PRAYER

God, thank You for listening to my prayers. Please help the people I love today. Amen.

Chapter 357: Being Thankful

"Give thanks in all circumstances." - 1 Thessalonians 5:18

God delights when we offer our thanks! Choosing to be grateful sharpens our eyes to the many blessings around us and reminds us of all God has done. Even in hard times, a thankful heart can find reasons to rejoice and hope to hold on to.

One simple way to grow gratitude is to keep a "thank-you" list each day. Share your list at dinner, in a conversation with a friend, or in a quiet moment of prayer. As you practice noticing and naming your blessings, thankfulness becomes a habit that brightens every day.

 **ACTIVITY**

Write down five things you're thankful for today.

_____

_____

_____

_____

_____

_____

_____

_____

_____

_____

PRAYER

Thank You, God, for all the blessings in my life. Help me to always have a thankful heart. Amen.

Chapter 358: Sharing Our Faith

"Always be ready to give an answer... for the hope that you have." - 1 Peter 3:15

Jesus wants us to tell others about Him. Sharing our faith doesn't have to be scary. It can be as simple as telling a friend, "Jesus loves you!" When we share our faith, we help others learn about God's love.

You can start by looking for everyday moments: a kind word when someone is upset, or inviting a friend to read a Bible story with you. Each small step opens a door for God's love to shine. As you practice sharing, you'll grow more confident, and you may be surprised how often a simple "Jesus loves you" can light up someone's day.

 ## ACTIVITY

Think of one friend you can tell about Jesus this week. Make a plan to do it!

 ## PRAYER

Jesus, help me to be bold and share Your love with others. Amen.

Chapter 359: Being a Good Example

"Set an example for the believers in speech, in conduct, in love, in faith and in purity." - 1 Timothy 4:12

People watch what we do, not just what we say. When we live like Jesus, we show others how to follow Him too. Being a good example means being kind, honest, and loving, even when no one is looking.

A simple way to shine Jesus' light is through small, everyday choices: holding the door for someone, speaking gently when you're upset, or admitting a mistake instead of hiding it. Each time you choose honesty over an easy lie or kindness over indifference, you build a bridge for others to see God's heart. Over time, those little acts add up and point people toward the love and truth you reflect.

 **ACTIVITY**

Think of one way you can be a good example today. Do it!

 **PRAYER**

God, help me to be a good example of Your love in everything I do. Amen.

Chapter 360: Serving Others

"Serve one another humbly in love." - Galatians 5:13

Jesus came to serve others, and He wants us to do the same. Serving means looking for ways to help people, giving our time and energy, and showing kindness without expecting anything back. When we serve others, whether it's carrying a friend's backpack, sharing our snack, or listening when someone needs to talk, we're putting God's love into action.

You can start by spotting one simple need each day: hold the door open, offer a smile to someone who seems lonely, or help a sibling with their chores. Serving doesn't require superpowers, just a willing heart. As you practice these small acts, you'll discover that serving not only brightens someone else's day, but also fills your own heart with joy and makes you more like Jesus.

 ACTIVITY

Find a way to serve someone today, like helping with chores or making a card for someone.

 **PRAYER**

Jesus, help me to serve others with a happy heart. Amen.

Chapter 361: Loving Our Neighbors

*"Love your neighbor as yourself." -
Mark 12:31*

Jesus said that loving our neighbors is one of the most important things we can do. Our "neighbor" is anyone around us: our friends, family, classmates, and even people we don't know well. Love means helping, listening, and caring.

When we pay attention to the people around us, seeing who needs a friend at lunch, who could use a hand with homework, or who just needs someone to listen, we're living out Jesus' command. Every small act of kindness and every moment we stop to really hear someone shows God's love in action and helps our neighborhoods become more like the family He intended.

 **ACTIVITY**

Do something kind for someone today to show love.

 **PRAYER**

Jesus, help me to love my neighbors just like You love me. Amen.

Chapter 362: Forgiving Others

"Forgive as the Lord forgave you." - Colossians 3:13

Forgiveness is choosing to let go of anger when someone hurts you. Jesus forgives us when we do wrong, and He wants us to forgive others too. Forgiving makes our hearts lighter and fills us with peace.

You can practice forgiveness by praying for the person who hurt you and choosing to let go of your anger. Every time you forgive, you share God's grace and open the door for healing in your own heart.

 ACTIVITY

Think of someone you need to forgive. Say, "I forgive you" in your heart.

 **PRAYER**

God, help me to forgive others like You forgive me. Amen.

Chapter 363: God's Promises for Our Future

"For I know the plans I have for you," declares the Lord. -Jeremiah 29:11

God has good plans for your life! Even when the future feels uncertain, we can trust that God is working for our good. He promises to guide us, love us, and be with us every step of the way.

When you feel unsure about what comes next, try this simple step: pause and talk to God about your hopes and worries. Remember times He's helped you before, big or small, and thank Him for those moments. As you look back on His faithfulness, your confidence in His good plans will grow, helping you step forward each day with courage and hope.

 # ACTIVITY

Draw a picture of a path with the sun shining above it.

PRAYER

God, thank You for having good plans for me. Help me trust You with my future. Amen.

Chapter 364: Heaven, Our Eternal Home

"He will wipe every tear from their eyes." - Revelation 21:4

One day, we will live with God forever in heaven! In heaven, there will be no more pain, sadness, or death. It will be full of joy, peace, and love. God is preparing a wonderful place for everyone who believes in Jesus.

Until that glorious day arrives, we can bring a taste of heaven into our world by showing kindness, offering forgiveness, and celebrating God's goodness in our daily lives. Every time we comfort someone who's hurting, choose gratitude in hard moments, or share a smile with a friend, we practice the joy, peace, and love that await us.

ACTIVITY

Draw a picture of a group of happy people.

PRAYER

Jesus, thank You for preparing a place for me in heaven. Help me live for You every day. Amen.

Chapter 365: Keep Growing in Faith!

"But grow in the grace and knowledge of our Lord and Savior Jesus Christ." - 2 Peter 3:18

Congratulations! You've spent 365 days learning about God, His love, and how to live for Him. Your journey isn't over, it's just beginning! Keep reading the Bible, praying, loving others, and growing closer to Jesus every day. God will be with you for the rest of your life.

Pause to celebrate the ways you've seen God work: answered prayers, moments of peace, and new growth in your heart. Share your favorite discoveries with a friend or family member, and consider starting another cycle or inviting someone else to join the adventure. Each new day is another chance to walk deeper, love stronger, and trust Him more as you continue following Jesus.

 ACTIVITY

Write down one way you will keep growing in faith this year.

_____

_____

_____

_____

_____

_____

_____

_____

_____

_____

PRAYER

Jesus, thank You for helping me grow in faith. Help me keep learning and loving You more every day. Amen.

Conclusion:
A Final Encouragement

You've finished a whole year of devotions. Remember, being a follower of Jesus is a lifelong adventure. Keep reading His Word, talking to Him in prayer, and sharing His love with others. When life is exciting or hard, Jesus is always with you. Keep growing, keep learning, and never forget how much God loves you. **This is just the beginning of your faith journey!**

Check out another book in the series

Welcome Aboard, Check Out This Limited-Time Free Bonus!

Ahoy, reader! Welcome to the Ahoy Publications family, and thanks for snagging a copy of this book! Since you've chosen to join us on this journey, we'd like to offer you something special.

Check out the link below for a FREE e-book filled with delightful facts about American History.

But that's not all - you'll also have access to our exclusive email list with even more free e-books and insider knowledge. Well, what are ye waiting for? Click the link below to join and set sail toward exciting adventures in American History.

Access your bonus here

https://ahoypublications.com/

Or, Scan the QR code!